D1249175

PATTON

★ THE | GENERALS ★

PATTON

The Pursuit of Destiny

★ THE | GENERALS ★

Agostino Von Hassell
and
Ed Breslin

THOMAS NELSON
Since 1798

NASHVILLE   DALLAS   MEXICO CITY   RIO DE JANEIRO

Published in Nashville, Tennessee, by Thomas Nelson. Thomas Nelson is a registered trademark of Thomas Nelson, Inc.

Thomas Nelson, Inc., titles may be purchased in bulk for educational, business, fund-raising, or sales promotional use. For information, please e-mail SpecialMarkets@ThomasNelson.com.

Library of Congress Cataloging-in-Publication Data

Von Hassell, Agostino.
    Patton : the pursuit of destiny / Agostino Von Hassell and Ed Breslin.
      p. cm.
    Includes bibliographical references and index.
    ISBN 978-1-59555-056-9
      1. Patton, George S. (George Smith), 1885-1945. 2. Generals—United States—Biography. 3. United States. Army—Biography. 4. World War, 1939–1945—Campaigns—Western Front. 5. World War, 1939–1945—Campaigns—Africa, North. 6. United States—History, Military—20th century. I. Breslin, Ed. II. Title.
    E745.P3V66 2010
    355.0092—dc22
    [B]   2010020129
Printed in the United States of America

10 11 12 13 14 WRZ 5 4 3 2 1

Contents

A Note from the Editor

To contemplate the lives of America's generals is to behold both the best of us as a nation and the lesser angels of human nature, to bask in genius and to be repulsed by arrogance and folly. It is these dichotomies that have defined the widely differing attitudes toward the "man on horseback," which have alternatively shaped the eras of our national memory. We have had our seasons of hagiography, in which our commanders can do no wrong and in which they are presented to the young, in particular, as unerring examples of nobility and manhood. We have had our revisionist seasons, in which all power corrupts—military power in particular—and in which the general is a reviled symbol of societal ills.

Fortunately, we have matured. We have left our adolescence

with its gushing extremes and have come to a more temperate view. Now, we are capable as a nation of celebrating Washington's gifts to us while admitting that he was not always a gifted tactician in the field. We can honor Patton's battlefield genius and decry the deformities of soul which diminished him. We can learn both from MacArthur at Inchon and from MacArthur at Wake Island.

We can also move beyond the mythologies of film and leaden textbook to know the vital humanity and the agonizing conflicts, to find a literary experience of war which puts the smell of boot leather and canvas in the nostrils and both the horror and the glory of battle in the heart. This will endear our nation's generals to us and help us learn the lessons they have to teach. Of this we are in desperate need, for they offer lessons of manhood in an age of androgyny, of courage in an age of terror, of prescience in an age of myopia, and of self-mastery in an age of sloth. To know their story and their meaning, then, is the goal here and in the hope that we will emerge from the experience a more learned, perhaps more gallant, and, certainly, more grateful people.

Stephen Mansfield
Series Editor, *The Generals*

Introduction

GENERAL GEORGE S. PATTON JR. was both blessed
and cursed in being the subject of one of the best biopics of all time.
When the movie *Patton* appeared in theaters in 1970, it caused a
sensation. George C. Scott's performance in the title role won him
an Academy Award for Best Actor. The movie also won Oscars for
Best Picture, Best Director, and Best Screenplay. By combining an
in-depth character study with the broad sweep of an epic, the movie
hit a nerve on two counts. It immortalized the best field general the
U.S. Army had in World War II, and it sanctified the heroic effort of
the American people in helping to win that monumental war. The
film blessed Patton by showcasing his inspirational leadership, his
logistical daring, and his battlefield brilliance.

The film cursed him, though, by distorting his personality,

exaggerating his character flaws, and sensationalizing his eccentricities. Each of these arose from the fact that a spiteful former rival, General Omar N. Bradley, served as the film's chief consultant. The sensationalizing of Patton's eccentricities resulted from typical Hollywood indulgence in dramatic license to achieve heightened effects. The result today is that it is hard to tell Patton the Myth from Patton the Man.

The story told here is that of Patton the Man. It does not neglect his serious shortcomings, but the emphasis is on his considerable virtues, not least his indisputable magnificence as a battlefield commander, master tactician, virtuoso trainer of troops, inspirational leader, and prescient expert on—and practitioner of—modern mobile armored warfare.

By the time the movie was made, Patton was already a famous general. His exploits were well publicized during his career. So, too, were his monumental political gaffes. As a larger-than-life character, Patton had virtues and faults that were both outsized. His mood swings were wide and prompted by deep fissures in his psyche. His demons were many and hideous, and their ability to disfigure him was large. Impulse control was a lifelong issue for him, as it is for many overly intense, impassioned people. He demanded a total commitment to excellence from himself and demanded this same commitment from everyone under his command.

Upon the movie's release in Great Britain, its full title was *Patton: Lust for Glory*. This subtitle implies that Patton was driven solely by egomania. That is patently untrue. The movie's negative emphasis on Patton's failings resulted from General Omar Bradley's ill will toward him. Bradley resented Patton on several counts, just as he resented British field marshal Bernard Law Montgomery. During World War II, Patton and Montgomery achieved spectacular victories, whereas Bradley never did. The former were vainglorious professional soldiers who reveled in recognition of their accomplishments. They loved every aspect of military life and effected flamboyance in sculpting their public images. Patton favored riding boots, jodhpurs, and a shiny silver helmet; Monty embraced a stylized beret set at a rakish angle, sweaters with leather shoulders, and a swagger stick under his armpit. Bradley, in contrast, was a self-effacing journeyman who wore standard-issue uniforms and reveled in his democratic touch, earning the nickname "the GI General." What hurt his image even more was having only one triumph, the breakout in Normandy in Operation Cobra. The success of Operation Cobra, however, resulted from Patton's—not Bradley's—daring aggression.

Together with German field marshal Erwin Rommel, Patton and Montgomery formed a trinity of celebrated generals who fought aggressively with cutting-edge equipment and techniques in the European Theater during World War II. Unlike them, Bradley was considered an administrator whose total grounding in infantry tactics precluded the innovative use of mobile armored warfare that distinguished the victories of Patton, Montgomery, and Rommel. Bradley was old-school, stodgy, and slow; they were cutting-edge, daring, and speedy. Bradley was inclined to stalemated standoffs; they favored quicksilver flanking, pincer, and enveloping checkmates.

The posthumous publication of Patton's memoir, *War as I Knew It*, made matters worse between Patton and Bradley. The book was based on Patton's private journals, letters, and diaries kept during the war. In them, he was critical of Bradley and of Eisenhower. Both of these generals outranked Patton when they saved his career after the various political crises resulting from Patton's impulsive and indiscreet actions or statements. This was especially true after the infamous incidents when Patton twice slapped battle-fatigued soldiers in Sicily in 1943. Such cruel and inappropriate behavior so outraged public opinion at home that an outcry arose in Congress to have Patton removed from command and returned home in disgrace.

To Bradley, Patton's memoir made Patton seem like the ultimate ingrate. In fact, he was not; he was simply a harsh taskmaster in all things military. He found Bradley wanting as a battlefield commander, strategist, and tactician; and because of Patton's integrity, he simply said so in his private writings. It was his widow, Beatrice, and not Patton, who approved publication of his private writings as a memoir. The implications in the movie that Patton was mercurial to the point of insubordination are not true. When Patton served under Bradley, he was intensely loyal, never insubordinate, carrying out orders even when he disagreed with Bradley's strategy and tactics.

The movie also indicts Patton, especially during the campaign in Sicily, for putting his ambition ahead of the lives and safety of the men serving under him, one of whom was Bradley. It is true that Patton's strategy as commander of the U.S. Seventh Army in the conquest of Sicily was extremely bold; he did want to beat General Montgomery and his British Eighth Army to Messina, vanquish the retreating German army, and claim primacy in the conquest of the island for the Allies. As an ardent student of military history, especially of classical and ancient military history, Patton did desire to add his name to the list of Sicily's famous conquerors. Yet this was not his only motivation. At the time he was tired of British criticism of the U.S. Army and its alleged ineptitude; he took personal umbrage at the British joke that the Americans were "our Italians," playing off the contempt the Germans voiced for the deficient fighting ability of their Italian allies. Patton resented the secondary and subsidiary role assigned to the Americans by the British commanders in the Sicily campaign. For this he blamed Eisenhower and did not go easy on him in the private writings that became *War as I Knew It*.

Statistics disprove the charge that Patton, in keeping with his nickname of "Old Blood and Guts," was reckless and cavalier where the lives and safety of his troops were concerned. The number of casualties under Patton's command throughout his career was remarkably low, a fact dramatically underscored when compared to the number of casualties he and his troops inflicted on the enemy. He was no "Butcher Joe" Hooker, the Union general who had to be relieved of command by President Lincoln early in the Civil War due to the appalling losses of life and limb incurred under his leadership. Patton exposed his men to only the briefest window of enemy fire, believing always that an attacking army was less vulnerable than a dug-in army. An attacking army offered fewer targets to the enemy.

A third flaw imputed to Patton by the movie was that he was a petty martinet. He was not. He was a thoroughgoing professional officer who was a stickler for military detail and protocol because he believed they reinforced battlefield discipline and prepared-ness and always bolstered morale. These virtues also promoted cohesiveness and instilled a greater sense of teamwork. That is why Patton insisted on military detail and protocol being hon-ored, from the shine of one's boots to the tightness of the knot in one's tie, to the erectness of one's posture and the snap in one's salute. He believed a soldier should be bursting with pride in his profession and in his unit.

Because of this belief, Patton set an unwavering example of correctness in all things military. As a former Olympic athlete and a world-class horseman and polo player, he kept himself physi-cally fit and in fighting trim and insisted on the same two qualities in everyone who served under him. In the same vein, he resented jibes from the British about the lack of professionalism in the U.S. Army early in World War II. Throughout his career, Patton also chafed at the jaundiced U.S. Marine Corps' view of the compara-tively lax and slovenly physical fitness requirements of U.S. Army regulars, including officers.

Patton's qualities of exemplary leadership, of sustained self-discipline, and unstinting professionalism placed him among the most effective trainers of troops in the history of the U.S. Army. His infectious example alone attracted loyalty and generated enthusiasm. From his days at West Point he set the tone for all of this. As regimental adjutant at the Point, he read the orders at the morning assembly and led the cadets whenever they marched. Later he devised the methods and wrote the literature for the teaching of swordsmanship, for the deployment of tanks in war-fare, for the training of tankers, and for the establishment of the

Desert Training Center in southeastern California near the small town of Indio. The Desert Training Center is still in operation and played an important role in the preparation of troops for combat in the Gulf War and in Operation Iraqi Freedom. Patton first used the Center to school the tankers he led to victory in 1942 in Tunisia over Rommel's battle-hardened Afrika Korps.

The movie's emphasis on Patton's attraction to military appurtenances such as swords, ivory-handled pistols, shiny steel helmets, campaign ribbons, ribbon sashes, riding boots, and jodhpurs distorted the simple fact that he loved everything about being a professional soldier. He took to soldiering as a sacred calling, as a vocational commitment as worthy of devotion and reverence as a summons to the clergy. He was not just interested in the outward, physical aspects of being a soldier; inwardly he studied the military from an early age, immersing himself in classical military history and studying the strategies and tactics deployed at famous battles. This interest endured and his studies continued throughout his life. He read military history voraciously, and he kept abreast of all developments in military technology, especially weaponry. He was conscientious about reading military journals and technological publications. The implication from the movie that he was an empty-headed military hotdog, a strutting showboat—all surface, no substance—is not accurate, a point underscored by the fact that his extensive personal library now resides at West Point.

Another misconception the movie reinforced is that Patton was impulsive in waging war. On the contrary, he was noted for his extensive use of military intelligence and for his application of historical precedents in his preparation of detailed battle plans. His battle plans were known for their clarity and thoroughness. Very quickly in World War II he grasped the full significance of the ENIGMA intelligence breakthrough, which allowed the Allies to read all German radio transmissions. He made extensive use of this intelligence in forming his strategy and tactics and writing up his battle plans. He was not, as his detractors implied, another impulsive Custer looking for his own Little Big Horn. His analysis and preparation augmented his ability to "read" a combat situation precisely. This instinctive ability of his was uncanny, almost preternaturally so. It amounted to a kind of genius.

Genius might be an apt word to apply to Patton. He immersed himself in one profession and in one field of endeavor and then excelled at it to an astonishing degree. After schooling himself in military history and steeping himself in military know-how and lore, he applied this knowledge on the battlefield. His knowledge of classical military history alone was so extensive that he made reference to it frequently, as he did, for instance, while fighting his way out of Normandy, across France, and into Germany in 1944. He cited roads that had been used by William the Conqueror and towns where famous Roman battles had been fought.

When he made these references, he often claimed to have been present for these historical events in former lives. His professed belief in reincarnation was emphasized in the movie. This belief, however, was not formative for him in his early life. He was brought up with traditional Christian values. Nor did he embrace any of the oriental religions for which reincarnation is a tenet. His avowed belief in reincarnation was more a theatrical affectation than a hard fact. Or, at most, it seemed to be a slight and harmless delusion, and one not clinically psychotic—it entailed no formal break with reality into a schizophrenic, or even a schizoid, state. It was more a flamboyant fantasy to dress out his fully articulated military persona, a mental accessory to the matching ivory-handled pistols, the shiny steel helmet, the polished riding boots, and the jodhpurs. In the movie a belief in reincarnation made for good theater.

So, too, did his kissing of the young officer leaning against the treads of the wrecked tank. The previous night the officer had survived a vicious tank battle that had deteriorated at the end into hand-to-hand combat. In their roles as armchair psychiatrists, movie reviewers in 1970 alleged that this scene carried with it homosexual implications for Patton. The record of his life bears this allegation out not one iota. Rather, during the extended period of peace between the two world wars, Patton, in his frustration and boredom, took to womanizing and drinking, to his and his family's detriment.

Yet another failing the movie alleged of Patton was political obtuseness. His entire career puts the lie to this. He shrewdly ingratiated himself with powerful people from the start and continued it to the end. Whether it was to the secretary of war or to a powerful superior officer, Patton formed alliances with the powerful and benefited from them. Like his forebears—professional military officers, lawyers and politicians, business and community leaders—Patton possessed an innate and keenly developed sense of diplomacy and political savvy in courting the favor of those positioned to advance his career. He availed himself of political adeptness except when his two demons appeared and overwhelmed his better judgment. That is when impulse control failed him and his hubris crippled what might have been.

His two great demons were fear of his own cowardice and the failure to stifle his detestation of Soviet communism. From early in his teens, Patton feared he might not be able to live up to the record of bravery and military heroism achieved by his family forebears. This accounts for his outsized admiration for courage under fire. In the case of slapping the two battle-fatigued soldiers in Sicily, there is no excuse for his behavior. His actions were reprehensible, worthy of condemnation.

There is, however, an explanation for it. His sense of duty and his deep affection for his troops would not allow Patton to forego visiting field hospitals full of the wounded, the mutilated, and the dying. As both Eisenhower and Bradley stated for the record, Patton had a sensitive nature. His letters to his wife confirm this. Patton confided to her that he dreaded field hospital visits but would not shirk them, as he would not shirk any aspect of his duty. A lesser man would have spared himself and skipped these hospital visits, as many superior officers did. Patton did not; he made the visits and pinned medals for bravery on the wounded and dying. This duty overstressed his sensibility and conjured his own fear of cowardice. The result was that he lashed out at men he incorrectly thought had succumbed to their cowardice and malingered while others paid the price.

For doing so he paid a steep price where it hurt the most. As a direct result of the slapping incidents, he lost his fighting command of the victorious Seventh Army in Sicily. While the rump of the Seventh was reduced to a small cadre under Patton's continuing command in Sicily, the bulk of its troops and equipment was reassigned to the Fifth Army on the Italian mainland under the command of Patton's rival General Mark W. Clark. Patton was left for almost a year to serve as a decoy, moved by Eisenhower around the Mediterranean and then around southeast England to keep the Germans guessing about the location of the inevitable next Allied assault. What was worse, Patton lost his chance to lead the next Allied assault as the top American field commander under Eisenhower's overall command. Instead the assignment of top American field commander went to General Bradley, Patton's former subordinate, who now reversed roles with him and became his commander. Patton did not get into the fighting in Normandy leading the Third Army until several weeks after the D-Day invasion.

Patton's demonic inability to at least temporarily censor his detestation of Russian communism—evidenced at his Knutsford luncheon speech in the spring of 1944 with an implied slight to the Soviets—led Eisenhower to doubt his discretion on sensitive issues. As a result, Eisenhower put him under a virtual gag order. The Knutsford speech, coming as it did only months after the slapping scandal had dominated headlines, moved many to believe that Patton was a man bent on career suicide. Luckily, this second scandal did not cost him his chance to fight on the Continent.

The Third Army's relief of Bastogne under Patton was the most spectacular logistical feat of the entire war. The performance in general of the Third Army was incredibly effective, from its inception in July 1944 right through V-E Day on May 8, 1945. The loyalty Patton commanded from his men over the course of that ten-and-a-half-month period has passed into lore. After the war, men who had served with him would state this fact proudly and often. Indeed, Frank McCarthy, the producer of the movie *Patton*, is eloquent proof of this pride and loyalty. Having served as an officer under Patton during World War II, McCarthy persisted for years against obdurate Hollywood resistance in order to get the movie finally made.

To assess Patton fairly, he must be understood fully. Apparently most of the men who served under him managed to do this. This short biography aims to make that possible for everyone. Despite his serious character flaws—the overstated machismo, the egregious use of foul language, the demonic lack of impulse control over his worst fear and over his most pronounced dislike—George Smith Patton Jr. was an outstanding American general. Through persistence and strength of will, despite handicaps and setbacks, many of them self-imposed, he was able to realize his lifelong goal to be a daring and courageous combat leader. In the end, he made a monumental contribution to a truly heroic victory in World War II.

Prologue

GENERAL GEORGE S. Patton Jr. believed he had a date with destiny. He did. It occurred during the holiday season in December 1944.

Nine days before Christmas that year, in the predawn hours of December 16, German field marshal Karl Gerd von Rundstedt hurled an army of 1.3 million troops at the Allied forces massed on the western front. The *Wehrmacht* troops were reinforced by troops drawn from the eastern front, by droves of teenaged recruits drawn from the Hitler Youth, and by the latest output of German industry, whose production of war matériel reached its peak that year.

The German attack that gloomy, frigid, and overcast morning caught the Allies flatfooted, taking them by total surprise. It should not have. For a week before the attack, local intelligence indicated the Germans were preparing an attack. Belgian shopkeepers, farmers, and assorted villagers discussed it. A stray Polish POW, who had been dragooned into the *Wehrmacht*, warned his Allied captors of a buildup. Belgian civilians, moreover, insisted that the Germans always attacked through the Ardennes, a forested region with rolling hills near the French border.

Allied commanders discounted this human intelligence. The Ardennes, they reasoned, was too heavily forested for dependable movement in winter—and the winter of 1944 was the coldest in Europe in ninety years. There was already much snow on the ground, and low-lying and heavily laden clouds threatened to bring more. Fog was nearly a constant, ice was scattered everywhere, mud was universal, frost showed up every morning, and the cold and wet conditions were debilitating, causing widespread frostbite, chilblains, trench foot, and diarrhea. In fact, these frigid and wretched conditions rendered certain places of the Ardennes impassable. How could advancing troops be resupplied and sustained when transport trucks had no access roads? And what, under these conditions, could the German Panther and Tiger tanks do on such primitive, narrow, and impaired roads?

Very little, thought Supreme Allied Commander Eisenhower and his close friend and confidant, General Omar N. Bradley. Eisenhower thus left the Ardennes only lightly defended, while making his top priority the Allied offensive thrust being made to the north of the region. The Allies concentrated their efforts on overrunning Aachen, the town on the edge of the Hurtgen Forest. British commander Bernard Law Montgomery had convinced

Eisenhower that this was the swiftest and most direct route to Berlin. Montgomery was certain that the Allies should throw maximum manpower and resources into the effort. But the battle there had been fought bitterly for the better part of six weeks, at a horrifying and pointless price in life and serious injury on both sides. The Allies had not been able to breach Germany's defensive Siegfried Line in order to set their caps for the Rhine, the point of the whole exercise.

The German generals agreed that the Ardennes presented a nonviable option for offensive warfare. They thought this for precisely the reasons Eisenhower and Bradley did: the weather and the inadequate roads made their chances of success unlikely.

But the supreme German commander disagreed. Adolf Hitler considered the unlikeliness of his Ardennes Offensive to be its greatest strength. He thought that this daring *Wehrmacht* counterthrust would change the entire complexion of the German geopolitical face-off with its three big enemies. The Americans, the British, and the Russians would be forced to blink. Hitler saw the counteroffensive as an opportunity to surprise the Allies. His crack panzer divisions could buckle the thin Allied line in the Ardennes, smash through it, then sprint all the way to Antwerp, the main port for Allied supplies. The offensive would also split the Allied armies into two camps, and replicate for the hated British the nightmare of Dunkirk four and a half years later.

Hitler, who had an overactive fantasy life when it came to scenarios of dominance and destruction, visualized the Western Allies stunned and smashed. With them quieted and broken in spirit, he could then rapidly redeploy his reinforced and reinvigorated

Wehrmacht back to the eastern front. Seeing the reconstituted and revitalized *Wehrmacht* once again up to strength, Stalin, according to Hitler's scheme, would sue for peace on the basis of a 1939 reprise of the division of Eastern Europe between the two dictatorships.

Hitler had been preaching and planning this counter offensive doctrine since September. He would not be deterred from it. To his generals' cries and pleas to consider the Reich's need for fuel and increased manpower and matériel to make all of this happen, Hitler repeated his ebullient answers of five years earlier, when his war machine had roared through first Poland on one frontier and then the Ardennes on the opposite frontier, conquering half of Europe in a matter of months with the speed, daring, and ruthlessness of *Blitzkrieg*. He promised tanks and rockets and jets. He vowed that the *Luftwaffe* would once again assert superiority in airpower, as it had in the heady days of fall 1939 and spring 1940.

To the overarching question of where the fuel would come from to power this modern war machine, Hitler calmly explained that the speed and daring of the attack would be such that captured Allied supplies and matériel would more than suffice to fill the bill. The German army would scythe down all resistance and capture the Allied stockpiles of gasoline, ammunition, food, and medical supplies. His generals had no option but to obey, disagree though they did.

Any student of Clausewitz and Sun-Tzu knows that the element of surprise is priceless in warfare and that the more daring the initiative, the more spectacular the payoff, should things work out as planned. The Führer was banking on this maxim holding true for him and the *Wehrmacht* one more time.

What Hitler failed to factor into his equation for triumph was the stouthearted bravery of the average GI and the preternatural genius for mobile armored warfare (*Blitzkrieg* by another name) of General George Smith Patton Jr. For three decades, Patton, an old cavalry officer, had studied the most effective use of armor, especially tanks. He knew how to deploy them swiftly to attack an enemy's weakness, halt his advance, penetrate his lines, fragment his troops, vanquish his artillery and armor, and force him to retreat.

Fortunately, Eisenhower knew what Patton could do. The Supreme Allied Commander had endured Patton's loutish behavior the previous summer in Sicily, when Patton infamously slapped two battle-fatigued privates in evacuation hospitals—an incident that nearly cost him his career. Eisenhower also had endured Patton's foolish behavior when, at a women's gathering at Knutsford, England, Patton had caused an international flare-up by speaking about the postwar geopolitical arrangement in a way that insulted the Russians by implying their exclusion. Moreover, clashes with other high-ranking Allied commanders made Patton a constant thorn in Eisenhower's side. Through it all, though, Eisenhower remained patient and wise, characterizing his friend of a quarter century as merely a "problem child." Eisenhower had stuck by him.

Patton was about to demonstrate why.

ONE

Bloodlines and Childhood

GEORGE S. PATTON Jr. was born on November 11, 1885, on a large family estate just outside Los Angeles, California. By his own admission, Patton had a great childhood. At one point he proclaimed himself the happiest boy in America. Lake Vineyard Rancho was an idyllic setting for a boy to grow up in, and young Patton had everything he needed to have a good time—plus the freedom and security to enjoy it. Besides the fact that the estate was vast and scenic, the adobe house built by his grandfather was large and filled most of the time with members of a loving and supportive family. Relatives encouraged Patton's interest in his ancestors, many of whom were high achievers in the military, in business, and in politics. In many ways, Patton is proof of the effectiveness of a happy childhood guided by loving parents and family members who worked hard to instill in him a set of values on which to base his entire life. These values derived from the landowning families prominent in colonial Virginia. Through his own privileged upbringing, he considered himself the embodiment of aristocratic military values often associated with the upper classes of Europe. More than any other single factor, this Virginia aristocratic tradition of pursuing a professional military career ignited young George's imagination from his earliest childhood and inspired him to dedicate his life to becoming a great military leader.

Patton's family had great military bloodlines on his paternal side and good ones on his maternal side. Patton was extremely proud of his antecedents, as he was of his pronounced Scots heritage, and he knew by heart the names of not just his direct forebears who had distinguished themselves as soldiers, but also the names of distant cousins, especially those who had served in the Civil War. In all, thirteen Patton men served in the War between the States. Three of them perished, including Patton's much admired and honored grandfather, Colonel George Smith Patton, who was head of the 22nd Virginia Regiment and was mortally wounded at the third battle of Winchester on September 19, 1864.

The first Patton in the colonies, however, was Robert Patton, George S. Patton Jr.'s great-great-grandfather. Born in Ayr, Scotland, on September 24, 1750, Robert Patton emigrated twenty years later from Glasgow and wound up in Culpeper, Virginia, where he went to work for a Scottish trading company. He prospered over the years to the point where he became one of the town's leading citizens. He initiated a Patton family tradition of marrying well when he took as his bride Anne Gordon Mercer, the daughter of Revolutionary War hero Brigadier General Hugh Mercer. Eventually the prosperous couple settled in Fredericksburg, Virginia, where they raised seven children.

Their third child was John Mercer Patton, Patton's great-grandfather. After graduating from the University of Pennsylvania in 1818, he practiced law in Fredericksburg, which he represented as a state congressman from 1829 to 1838. He spoke his mind and became embroiled in many controversies, including the national banking controversy that erupted when President Andrew Jackson attempted to overhaul and recharter the Bank of the United States. In what became a family trait, he stood his ground and never flinched in the face of a fight. When the incumbent governor of Virginia resigned in 1841, for thirteen brief days John Mercer Patton served as acting governor of the Commonwealth.

John Mercer Patton married Margaret French Williams, a notoriously strong-willed woman from another upper-tier colonial Virginia family. They produced a dozen children, seven of whom would serve in the War between the States in the Confederate army. Among them was the first George Smith Patton, the grandfather hero of George S. Patton Jr. Colonel George Smith Patton set an indelible example of heroism when, wearing the Confederate gray, he was mortally wounded fighting for a cause he passionately believed in.

Patton's grandfather entered the Virginia Military Institute (VMI) in 1849. Three years later, he graduated second in his class overall and first in French, mathematics, Latin, geology, chemistry, and tactics. The high mark in tactics was an inspiration for his grandson's subsequent tactical combat genius.

After graduating from VMI, he became a lawyer in his father's office. On November 8, 1855, he married Susan Thornton Glassell, the love of his life. She came from a family with a direct link to George Washington's great-grandfather, King Edward I of England. Her family could also point to such indirect forebears as King Philip III of France, and, even further back, to an affiliation with sixteen barons who signed the Magna Carta.

George Smith Patton settled his family in Charleston, Virginia. He practiced law until the Civil War broke out in 1861. In Charleston, he acquired the nickname "Frenchy" because he sported a goatee, dressed like a dandy, and acted in every way like a dashing cavalier, exhibiting classic chivalric behavior toward the opposite sex. Anecdotes of this behavior deeply affected his grandson, whose lifelong penchant for flamboyance would distinguish—and sometimes plague—him wherever he went.

George Smith Patton entered the war as a lieutenant colonel in charge of the 22nd Virginia Regiment, serving under Thomas Jonathan "Stonewall" Jackson. The two men had an inauspicious start. Patton had studied under then-Professor Jackson at VMI, where the cadets dubbed the future Confederate general "Tom Fool" because he endeavored to teach artillery at the same time he was learning it, a circumstance that led to some awkward moments for the neophyte instructor. George Smith Patton nonetheless liked Professor Jackson and was later privileged to serve under him while head of the 22nd Virginia Regiment.

George Smith Patton was often accused of being arrogant but had the foresight and political moxie to see the clouds of war gathering early on. As a result, he had formed a militia group in Charleston known as the Kanawha Riflemen, named for the home county in which Charleston is located. The Riflemen attracted like-minded young aristocrats and, once the conflict began, evolved into the 22nd Virginia Regiment that George Smith Patton led into battle under Stonewall Jackson.

The two VMI men distinguished themselves at VMI's finest moment of the entire conflict, the battle of New Market. Two hundred forty-seven young cadets were pressed into action at that battle where Professor Jackson famously exclaimed, "Today the Institute will be heard from!" It was heard from indeed, and the heavily outnumbered Confederates won a fierce battle that entered VMI lore and legend. Any visitor to VMI today can see the rolling cannons used by the VMI cadets at New Market standing proudly on the edge of the main parade ground against the backdrop of the rolling Blue Ridge Mountains.

The victory at New Market was also the high-water mark for the Patton family during that all-out internecine war. George Smith Patton distinguished himself as a gifted battle leader with outstanding tactical instincts. With uncanny anticipation of an enemy move, he made a defensive adjustment early in the battle that completely thwarted a Union cavalry charge meant to roll up the Confederates' left flank. The men under Patton were full of admiration for his ability and his bravery. George Smith Patton was wounded in several battles throughout the war before he suffered a fatal gunshot wound at the Third Battle of Winchester in September 1864.

George Smith Patton's younger brother, Waller Tazewell Patton, also graduated from VMI in 1856. He, too, distinguished himself in the War between the States. "Taz" had been badly wounded at Second Bull Run, but managed to recuperate and return to his unit. There, as commander of the Seventh Virginia Infantry, he met his end as part of Pickett's Charge at Gettysburg, one of the seven thousand men—included in that fourteen-thousand-man charge—who perished within minutes of the horn sounding. Taz was mortally shot in the mouth as he leaped a stone wall leading the charge. In addition, two other brothers, Hugh Mercer Patton and James French Patton, enrolled while still in their teens and both went on to become lieutenants wounded in battle. Both were fortunate enough to survive the war.

The heroism of George Smith Patton and Uncle Waller Tazewell loomed large in the affections of the former's son, born George William Patton before the outbreak of the war in 1856. He, in turn, passed this affection on to his son, the famous grandson and great-nephew of these two fallen Civil War heroes. Interestingly enough, in Old English the name Patton means "from the warrior's manor."

Although Patton's father's original name was George William Patton, with his mother's permission he later changed it to George Smith Patton II, to honor both his heroic father and his stepfather, George Hugh Smith. The name change on the part of her firstborn is how George Smith Patton Jr., hero of the Bulge and Bastogne, came to be known as "Junior."

Like George Smith Patton, George Hugh Smith was also a genuine Civil War hero. After the conflict, he fled to Mexico rather than pledge allegiance to the federal government in Washington DC. He stayed in Mexico until passions cooled and then drifted north into Southern California, where he married George Smith Patton's widow, who had moved west with the financial aid of her brother.

After growing up in Los Angeles with his mother and stepfather, Patton's father enrolled at VMI, like his father and his uncles before him. He excelled both as a student and as an officer within the student corps. He was the highest-ranking cadet officer in his senior class and was nominated as first captain. He was also exceptionally debonair, handsome, and a spellbinding public speaker, a trait he would pass along to his son.

His student years at VMI, however, were financially trying, and he was often embarrassed by his poverty. His stepfather earned a decent living as a lawyer, but he and his wife had two additional children of their own, making six children for whom they had to provide. This did not leave much money to expend on their son back east at VMI.

After he graduated in 1877, Patton's father spent another year at VMI as an instructor in French and tactics. Like the majority of Pattons, he felt himself most at home in Virginia and would have preferred to remain there. But his sense of duty to his mother and family forced him to return to Los Angeles, where he took up the study of law under the tutelage of his uncle and his stepfather. In

1880, after passing the bar, he joined the family firm and started to practice law.

At that time Los Angeles was a boomtown. Fortunes were being made, especially through the railroads. The Southern Pacific Railroad was the chief power in town, a strong monopoly in a young city that sprouted many powerful monopolies. Along with boom times and monopolies came corruption and power politics. With his great gift for oratory, Patton's father stepped right into this maelstrom. In 1884, he went on the stump for presidential candidate Grover Cleveland, who won the election and became the first Democratic president since the outbreak of the Civil War.

George S. Patton Jr.'s maternal bloodlines were equally illustrious. The exposure Patton's father won in campaigning for President Grover Cleveland brought him continued publicity and raised his civic profile. He was a young man about town, a desirable bachelor. His exposure won him the attention of Ruth Wilson, whom he married shortly after the election in 1884. Ruth was the daughter of Benjamin Wilson—a powerful landowner and businessman, a former frontiersman, fur trapper, bear hunter, Indian fighter, explorer, adventurer, and real estate speculator—who was one of the founders of Los Angeles. Wilson was the owner of the vast estate called Lake Vineyard Rancho on which his famous World War II hero of a grandson would be born a year after the marriage.

Benjamin Wilson was the son of a Revolutionary War hero and early pioneer who had moved west after that war ended. In

California, his power earned him the title "Don Benito" from the prosperous Mexican families prominent in the area. He was elected the first mayor of Los Angeles, a position he used to help establish the seaport of Wilmington, south of the city, and to found the city of Pasadena. He also served two terms in the California state legislature.

Benjamin Wilson was a truly larger-than-life character, and many aspects of his life read like tall tales. He became entangled with the Apaches in New Mexico, with whom he traded on friendly terms until that relationship turned sour and they condemned him to death. Only with the help of an Apache chief was he able to escape, half-naked and pursued by Apache braves, back to Santa Fe. He was also nearly killed in a fight with a grizzly bear that was preying on his cattle. He would not give up on killing this bear, despite being mauled badly in their first encounter. He stalked it through two more encounters before finally killing it. So wild was his temper, and so intense his inability to brook nonsense and suffer fools, that he refused to carry a sidearm for fear of using it rashly.

Ruth Wilson was the younger of Wilson's two daughters. When she married George Patton, it was a major social event in the City of Angels and captured local newspaper headlines. A year later, on November 11, 1885, she and her husband became the proud parents of a young son, christened George Smith Patton Jr. The boy was named in honor of his grandfather and father and, through the use of Smith as a middle name, in honor of the newborn's step-grandfather, George Hugh Smith. Throughout the boy's childhood, Smith would regale him with tales of his grandfather George S. Patton's Civil War heroism. The child was steeped in military lore from his earliest days.

Lake Vineyard Rancho provided a fertile setting for Patton's lifelong military passion. His father was determined to raise his son as a Virginia gentleman and cavalier, even though he was some twenty-five hundred miles west of the Old Dominion. Patton learned to ride as a toddler, and he had his own pony when he was scarcely old enough to sit on it. Weapons, too, were introduced early on, with the gift from his father of a .22-caliber rifle. From an early age Patton would prowl the large estate, shooting at small game. Young Patton was a good marksman, and he pleased and astonished his family by knocking an orange off a fence with his .22 when still a stripling.

Patton's childhood love of guns and rifles accounts for his signature characteristic as a general of carrying his greatly loved twin ivory-handled pistols with him at all times when in uniform. He spent his boyhood in America, right before the turn of the twentieth century, at a time when the stories of Rudyard Kipling were all the rage for young boys, when Captain Marryat's tales of adventure similarly held sway, and, slightly later, when Teddy Roosevelt and his Rough Riders would make headlines in Cuba during the Spanish-American War. The lore of the modern man of action extolled by Kipling, Marryat, and the example of Teddy Roosevelt would coalesce with the traditions of the

Southern cavalier to mold Patton's personality, passions, aspirations, and dreams.

Patton's hunger for tales of heroes and warfare was fed by his father's habit of reading aloud to him from the novels of Sir Walter Scott, a staple of the Southern gentry, which featured intrepid and noble knights. His father also read to him from Shakespeare's great tragedies and from classics of strife and triumph, like Homer's *Iliad* and *Odyssey*. These tales of great adventure and of stirring leaders would impact Patton the rest of his life, influencing his adult habit of reading history, especially military history.

Two visitors to the Patton household also enthralled young George with tales of bravery and derring-do. One was his step-grandfather, George Hugh Smith. The other was an even more celebrated hero of the Civil War, John Singleton Mosby, who after the war practiced law on the staff of the Southern Pacific Railroad in Los Angeles. Mosby, like the Pattons and like Smith, was one of many disenchanted Southerners who migrated west to Southern California after the South's bitter defeat, unable to abide conditions at home and the dominance of the victorious federal government in nearby Washington DC. Known as the "Gray Ghost" for his feats as a guerrilla cavalry officer, Colonel Mosby mesmerized young George with tales of daring cavalry raids carried out during the war.

Patton's father reinforced his son's interest in things military by teaching him how to build forts and by fashioning for him wooden swords with which to play war games and pantomime duels. This instilled in Patton an interest in swordsmanship that would become a hallmark of his life, culminating in his participation in fencing at the Olympics. Patton's younger sister and only sibling, nearly two years his junior, Anne "Nita" Wilson Patton, became Patton's sole charge in these childhood war games. Her role was subservient, of course, as a trooper to her favored brother's officer. He spent his time snapping commands and directing mock battles. As the children grew older, the games became more elaborate and involved other playmates. But no matter how large the contingent grew, Patton remained in charge. In later life, when interviewed about her famous brother, Nita joked that he always assigned her the role of the vanquished foe.

Patton had a great boyhood companion named Ignacio "Nacho" Callahan. From the time the two boys were about eight or ten years old, they had the run of the eighteen-hundred-acre estate on their ponies. Patton's was a stout Shetland named Peach Blossom, not much of a moniker for an imagined warhorse, but Patton and Nacho also played childhood games of polo that led years later to another lifelong passion for the general: playing competitive polo at the highest levels. The two boys also swam in a swamp, and quite often they rustled Patton's father's cattle, horses, and mules.

Patton's father was industrious during his son's childhood, working himself to a frazzle whenever that became mandatory to support his family in the style he deemed appropriate to their station in life as transplanted Virginia aristocrats. When the many businesses left to the family by Benjamin Wilson foundered and nearly collapsed under mismanagement, Patton's father was forced to essentially abandon his budding career as a lawyer and politician and return to Lake Vineyard to direct all family business enterprises.

This salvage job immersed him in business affairs to such an extent that his son came to resent it. Patton's time with his father was curtailed. This was doubly sad because his father was determined to raise his son to achieve the dreams he had had to forfeit in the face of his mother's and his siblings' domestic needs. Patton Sr. was never able, like his father and stepfather before him, to cash in on his VMI education and his heroic patrimony and attain military glory. He badly wanted his son to not suffer the same fate of watching his dreams and destiny shorted. As a result, Patton's father transferred his own dreams to his boy and doted on him, referring to him always and exclusively as "the boy" or as "my hero son."

Patton's father may have inadvertently imposed a hardship on his son while Patton was still very young. Patton Sr. had some unorthodox ideas about the education of children, believing it should be carried out in languid stages and that basic skills in reading and writing were not an essential foundation to be established first. As much fun as young Patton was having on the vast family ranch, he was not compelled by law to attend school in those pre-regulated days. This meant—though he absorbed such classics of literature as Homer's *Iliad* and *Odyssey*, Plutarch's *Lives*, the novels of Sir Walter Scott, and vast passages of the Bible, among many other worthy books read aloud to him—he never learned how to decipher the printed page, let alone how to write or spell until he was twelve years old, quite an advanced age for acquiring basic reading and writing skills.

As a result, he was challenged and severely disadvantaged when he did finally start attending a formal school in 1897. He went to the Classical School for Boys in nearby Pasadena, where Patton—despite the strain—took avidly to reading about such heroes of antiquity as Alexander the Great, Hannibal, Constantine, Julius Caesar, and Themistocles, fortifying yet again his thirst to know more about kings, conquerors, villains, famous warriors, and great generals.

Because of Patton's late start with basic reading, writing, and arithmetic skills, many biographers have written that he suffered from dyslexia. Patton had difficulty reading aloud throughout his life and never managed to master the art of spelling. But as Stanley P. Hirshson theorized persuasively in his recent biography, *General Patton: A Soldier's Life*, Patton was not so much dyslexic as deprived. Despite his late start, moreover, he was quite successful at schoolwork. He did well in mathematics, usually a stumbling block for the dyslexic, and he loved history and learned fairly quickly to read it well. English did not present any insurmountable problems; he even learned to spell the words given to him in class.

Patton's deficient education had three notable impacts on him that presented challenges he had to meet and setbacks and embarrassments he had to overcome. First, reading aloud in class especially embarrassed him and left him vulnerable to barbs from his class-mates. But that was minor compared to the second challenge when—as a late teenager—he applied for the military education he had sought since his earliest years, he was at a severe disadvantage on the competitive tests. His father contemplated sending him to a prep school in Morristown, New Jersey, that specialized in preparing students for the service academies. After much contemplation, however, Patton's father followed family tradition and sent young George back east for a year of prep at VMI, with an eye to building George up for admission to West Point.

The third and hardest challenge came two years later. It also had the most embarrassing impact on Patton. After successfully completing his year of prep work at VMI, Patton managed to gain admittance to West Point. He spent a difficult plebe year there, only to be forced to repeat his first-year studies because of academic deficiencies. This setback embarrassed him, and he spent a difficult summer in 1905 brooding about it.

These setbacks are important for reasons that cannot be emphasized enough. First, whenever Patton encountered a setback in life, he did not quit. He persevered until he met the challenge and solved the problem. Even as a young student, when other students laughed at his wretched inability to read aloud, he kept at it until he acquired the skill, despite the discomfort.

Second, from being read to so long into his childhood, Patton learned to be a good listener. More important, he developed a good memory. As a child he memorized large segments of writing and could recite them verbatim. His ability to retain historical facts and to memorize the strategic and tactical details of historic battles was legendary. This facility at memorizing and retaining large blocks of information aided his planning of battles; it also sharpened his ability to adjust to circumstances during these battles and take brilliant countermeasures. As a commander, Patton was a stickler for intelligence on the enemy, including troop strength and disposition, number of tanks and other armored vehicles, extent of artillery available, strength of air support, and other vital factors. Almost effortlessly he could file this information away and draw on it as needed.

Third, because Patton was loved and nurtured so intensely by his parents and other family members, he never lost confidence in himself. No matter the humiliation, he bounced back. His father promoted his confidence no matter what happened. When Patton had difficulties in school, his father assured him he was doing well and could do better, if only he stayed with it. His mother reinforced his self-worth at all times, minimizing failures, maximizing successes. Moreover, his aunt Nannie devoted her life to Patton, considering him her surrogate son. She read to him profusely when he was a small boy. She especially read him everything she could put her hands on about Napoleon, who fascinated young George from the time he was a toddler. Most important, she read to the youngster voluminously and frequently from the Bible. He had a prodigious memory for Scripture his entire life. Biographer Carlo D'Este points out in *Patton: A Genius for War* that Patton once contested his friend Francis Spellman, then archbishop of New York, for knowledge of the Bible, and won, just as D'Este reports that Patton also won against a Harvard historian when the two matched wits on knowledge of historical facts.

His religious upbringing is another key to understanding Patton. He was steeped in Christian theology and values from his earliest days, and loved it when Aunt Nannie would read to him *The Pilgrim's Progress*. One of his favorites, the book emphasizes perseverance against adversity and the embrace of spiritual values and a higher cause. In the Southern tradition, the Bible was the most important book in the Patton household. That Patton later debated theology and history with acknowledged experts in these fields shows again his unshakable confidence, nurtured and couched in the oral, not the literary, tradition. In both instances of matching wits with experts in their fields, Patton was engaged verbally and dependent on memory only, not on texts or on written briefs or arguments.

The same talents fueled his oratorical gifts. Like any great orator, he did not read his speeches. In most cases, he did not even write them down. He gave his speeches without script or notes, and even taught classes on tank warfare using only short notes and sometimes only jotted a few words on index cards to jog his memory. He would glance down at these notes, then look back up, maintain eye contact with his audience, and continue his monologue.

In overcoming the early obstacles to achieving his goals, Patton's happy childhood guided by a loving family instilled in him a set of values on which he based his entire life. He came from people used to assuming responsibility in the political, commercial, academic, and military realms, and he learned from them how to be steadfast in the face of adversity, how to remain calm and decisive in a crisis, and how to avoid despair by conspiring with his faith to convert any negative to a positive.

That Patton remained religious as well as spiritual his whole life is often not given the prominence it deserves in accounting for his ultimately successful and triumphant career. Despite his many personality and character flaws, despite his unfortunate predilection for profanity, and despite his regrettable warmongering tendencies, he prayed to his God throughout his life and maintained throughout his military career a close relationship with the chaplains assigned to him and his forces. In the fall of 1944, he even decorated the Third Army chaplain with a Bronze Star for composing a prayer for good weather so Patton and his forces could wage war effectively and, as Patton himself phrased it, "kill Germans." He would often pray with his chaplains on the eve of battle, as he did on board ship the night before the invasion of Sicily, and he took counsel with his God and prayed for courage, strength, and success on most important occasions. He always retained his boyhood habit, taught to him by his mother, Ruth, of kneeling to pray, and he kept a Bible with him wherever his career postings and military campaigns took him.

TWO

Military Education

A S   M U C H   A S   Patton prized the military life and family heritage and tradition, it was wise of his father to dispatch him to VMI in the fall of 1903. The previous year, Patton's father had badgered California senator Thomas R. Bard to have his son appointed to West Point. That political appointment did not materialize, and Patton Sr. decided that young George must improve his academic standing and his ability as a student in order to be competitive for the senatorial appointment. He wrote to the superintendent of VMI and explained his son's situation. The superintendent understood and accepted Patton for enrollment that fall of 1903, fully cognizant that the young man was committed to academic self-improvement that would propel him the following year to West Point.

In early September of that year, Patton's father, mother, sister Nita, and Aunt Nannie accompanied him east by train to Lexington, Virginia, and installed him at his father and grandfather's alma mater. Patton loved VMI instantly and took to the military life with maximum zeal. Right from the start he was a martinet when it came to procedures and military manners, following assiduously the rules of comportment and the strict dress code for first-year VMI cadets, then, as now, called "rats." When he visited the school's tailor, Patton was pleased to learn that his uniform measurements exactly matched those of his father and of his Civil War–hero grandfather. Always mindful of tradition, Patton also noted that the cadet captain who initiated him officially into the school occupied the same honored room, just inside the main portal, that his father had lived in when he was cadet captain more than a quarter century earlier.

Patton did not receive a single demerit during his year at VMI. He worked hard as a scholar, improved his academic record significantly, and received word from home that Senator Bard had invited him in February to participate in the competitive examinations for appointment in June 1904 to West Point. General Scott Shipp, the superintendent of VMI, granted Patton a leave of absence to travel to Los Angeles and take the tests. Patton left immediately by train for the six-day journey, studying diligently along the way. When he reached Los Angeles, he and his father were riddled with anxiety. The next day, however, young George showed up, took the tests, and came out on top. A month later the senator officially notified Patton that he had the appointment. Both father and son were ecstatic. Slow and reluctant as Senator

Bard had been to appoint Patton to West Point, it is ironic that it is the one deed in his whole tenure in office that he is remembered for today.

When Patton returned to VMI from his West Coast trip, the upperclassmen rode him mercilessly. The rivalry and animosity with West Point formed a staple of the collective psychological makeup of VMI, and the VMI cadets resented what they considered Patton's desertion of them. Patton endured it nobly and resigned from VMI on June 1. General Shipp hated to see him go. Patton had been an exemplary "rat" to such an extent that he was told, had he stayed for his second VMI year, he would have been appointed first corporal of his class, an honor accorded its top cadet. Yet Patton left, free of any regret or remorse. On the contrary, he knew West Point was going to tax his abilities to the fullest and couldn't wait to tackle the new challenge that lay ahead.

Besides his admittance to West Point, another momentous event had occurred in Patton's life, though he was not yet fully aware of its significance. Two years earlier, during the summer of 1902, when his father first approached Senator Bard about the West Point appointment, the Pattons had received visitors from Boston named Ayer. Frederick Ayer was a wildly successful self-made man. He had amassed a fortune in various businesses, principally in the soda business and the patent medicine business. Called by some the Sarsaparilla King, he marketed a soft drink called Cherry Pectoral, which, in fact, wasn't so "soft." Each bottle contained one-sixteenth of a grain of heroin.

When the Ayers came west that summer, they spent time with the Pattons at a house they had built on Catalina Island, which Patton Sr. and his partners hoped to turn into a classy resort. What this meant to young George was more privilege. He summered on the island and learned to sail, a pastime for which he developed a lifelong enthusiasm. He was also able to expand his scope as a hunter, roaming the hills and shooting wild goats. But the life-changing event that summer of 1902 was meeting Beatrice Ayer. Both were seventeen years old. The Ayers' oldest child was a sought-after Boston debutante who, despite her tender years, had already received—and refused—two marriage proposals. She was so physically beautiful and financially endowed that she drew a herd of suitors, one of them a Russian count. She loved to ride horses, gallop in the fox hunt, play polo, race yachts, shoot skeet, ski, ice-skate, and play tennis. She did all this despite being nearsighted and refusing to wear spectacles lest they diminish her beauty. Patton liked her habit of taking reckless dares in stride, like jumping and showing horses and even racing them across open country.

Neither Patton nor Beatrice knew they were smitten that magical summer, but when Beatrice returned to Boston in the fall the two started to correspond. Each had met the love of their life, but destiny swings on small hinges, and neither realized just how large and significant a door had been opened into their shared future. Besides, above all things, Patton had to devise a means to get admitted to West Point, his overriding ambition at the time, despite whatever his heart prompted him to feel.

All through his one year at VMI, Patton corresponded with Beatrice. Mostly he told her of his plans and dreams for the future; she in turn advised and encouraged him. By the time he entered West Point the following year, he wrote to her with increased regularity and had managed to see her for a few short visits at her family's residences in Massachusetts. Tellingly, when his first year at West Point challenged his mettle and tested his character to the utmost, he confided more in Beatrice. By now, despite the difficulties Patton experienced in learning spelling, grammar, and punctuation, his letters were mostly clear and precise. While marred by mistakes, his letters nevertheless show an understanding of composition and a feel for language.

Although he showed an outstanding aptitude for the military and distinguished himself for spit and polish, for marching, for bracing, and for overall military comportment, Patton encountered devastating problems with his studies, especially with mathematics, English, and French. Throughout that plebe year he struggled mightily and in letter after letter to his father confided his crippling fears that he would be a failure and never graduate. Each reply from his father minimized his shortcomings and encouraged him. To Patton's credit he redoubled his efforts.

In the end, however, his fears materialized and he was forced to redo his first year. Mercifully, in those days at West Point, when a plebe had to repeat his first year, he did not have to undergo yet another year of plebe hazing from upperclassmen. The cadet forced to repeat his first year was treated in military terms as an upperclassman but in academic terms as a plebe. This was a good thing, because Patton had endured a year of hazing as a "rat" at

VMI only to undergo a year of hazing as a "plebe" at West Point. During that year of hazing at West Point, he bore up well under it until his studies began to frustrate him in the extreme and he broke down and complained in a letter to his father that he could scarcely accommodate any more harassment from upperclassmen.

After learning he would need to repeat the first year's curriculum, Patton went home and summered with his family at their cottage on Catalina Island. He tried that summer through voluntary study to prepare himself better for the academic challenges that lay ahead in his second year, but spent a good portion of his time hunting and sailing as well. He did not like being a continent apart from Beatrice and feared his academic troubles would cost him her love.

If he failed to graduate from the Point, he believed she would reject him for a more distinguished and successful suitor. He failed to realize that she was deeply in love with him. Before he returned to West Point in the fall, he requested and was granted a visit of several days with Beatrice and her family at their summer residence in Beverly, Massachusetts. His time with her during that visit so exhilarated him that he left for West Point determined he would not fail.

Patton applied himself hard to his reprise of the first-year curriculum and met the challenges with success. In most subjects he managed to stay in the top third of his class and, importantly, managed to not flunk any of them. He also expanded his participation in athletics. He tried out again for the football team and, unlike the previous year, made it, though he was relegated to the third-string as an end. He also tried out for and made the track team; he was a good hurdler, but accident-prone. A third area of athletic endeavor was in fencing, where he excelled. As an aristocratic snob, Patton took to fencing with zeal; participation in this sport was traditionally restricted to well-born gentlemen only, and that pleased Patton's vanity immensely. Besides, he had loved swordplay even as a child with the simple wooden swords his father had fashioned for him. It's not surprising that he would go on to distinguish himself as a fencer in the Olympics and later in his army career would earn the title "Master of the Sword." In that capacity, as a young officer he designed a sword for the U.S. Army that to this day is called "the Patton sword."

This second year at West Point set a precedent for the three years to follow. Patton acquitted himself well academically and excelled to the utmost in things military. He also continued his involvement in athletics and, despite not being popular with many cadets because of his arrogance and snobbishness, in February 1908 earned the distinguished position of class adjutant. His military posture was excellent, his dress code beyond reproach. As adjutant, he stood each morning before the assembled cadets and read the orders of the day. Even better, whenever they marched, he would be out in front leading them.

Patton's fifth and final year at West Point was a triumph. At the annual Field Day, he set a new record in the 220-yard high hurdles, won the 120-yard high hurdles, and finished second in the 220-yard dash. He lettered in track and was proud his life long of his coveted *A*. In marksmanship he shot well enough to earn the designation "Expert," and in swordsmanship he continued to be outstanding. His horsemanship, as expected from having grown up riding from an early age on the ranch, was superb. Academically, he finished well. Yet he never became popular and never formed a close friendship among any of his 102 classmates. They considered him too full of himself and disliked his stated ambition to be a great general; they felt he should have kept such boasts to himself. He was also disliked for being a "quilloid," which in West Point jargon applied derogatorily to a guy too quick to grab a quill and write up a fellow cadet for an infraction. Patton's commitment to discipline was maniacal and off-putting for his fellow cadets.

Beatrice agreed with Patton's classmates. By now Patton was deeply in love with her, and his letters grew far more frequent and intimate. He confided in her more than ever. She felt comfortable enough to chide him gently for the same egotistical tendencies his classmates disliked. She pointed out that his letters were too full of "I this" and "I that." By now Patton was holding nothing back about his dreams to be a great and heroic military leader, and it could become a mite odious and grandiose. For someone who had trouble with grammar and spelling, Patton wrote prodigiously. He was impervious to her admonishments to be more reserved and humble; they had no impact.

From the time of his sad summer of 1905, Patton augmented his output of letters with notebooks and diaries in which he set down his innermost thoughts, feelings, dreams, ambitions, doubts, and desires. Importantly, he also elaborated his expanding philosophy on life in general and on the ingredients of leadership and greatness in particular, especially as they applied in the military realm. In his last year at West Point he even started to write poetry. He never discarded anything he wrote, believing it to be historically significant. About this he was right.

In his final year at West Point, he did something highly revelatory and completely foolish on the firing range. Assigned to work the pits, where he was busy raising, lowering, and marking targets, he suddenly stood up while those practicing kept shooting. Live bullets whizzed around him. Luckily he was unharmed. He did this as a self-imposed test of courage because he feared he lacked the fabled Patton bravery.

Six years earlier, on the eve of departing Southern California for VMI, on a walk with his uncle Andrew Glassell, he had confided his fears that he might be a coward. It was a growing preoccupation of his that would haunt him right to the end of his life. His uncle had replied that such a thing was not possible for a Patton. When Patton later told his father of this conversation, his father counseled him that while generations of gentility such as he possessed might make a man like him reluctant to engage in fisticuffs, such a well-bred man would gladly face death from weapons with a smile. Patton quickly internalized this observation as holy writ.

But it did not shield Patton from internal doubts, and for years he was accused of taking unnecessary and foolhardy risks, even by his World War II superior and friend Eisenhower. These internal doubts about his virility and courage go a long way to explain the coarse persona Patton projected for the first time during his cadet years at West Point. This persona ultimately grew into an obsession with machismo behavior that marred Patton's mature years, when his swagger was risibly exaggerated and his excessive use of profanity became disgusting.

In this failing he was much like Ernest Hemingway, a literary icon obsessed with the military just as Patton was a military icon obsessed with the literary. Both men were from privileged and pampered late-Victorian upper-middle-class backgrounds steeped in religious observance for which such behavior as they adopted was anathema. In both men of genius, close contact with proscribed lower-class behavior aroused in them the fear that they were sissies.

This fear of being a sissy was intensified not only by their privileged and "soft" childhoods but also by their superior intelligence and sensibility. Like Hemingway as a young reporter in Paris, Patton at West Point took up the writing of poetry as an outlet for his creativity and sensitivity. Like Patton, Hemingway recklessly courted death to prove himself brave. Under bombardment at a French farmhouse in World War II while working as a war correspondent, Hemingway sat helmet-less at a kitchen table even as everyone else, including high-ranking officers, retreated to the safety of the root cellar. Such "courage" as this—or standing up on a firing range—is arguably insane behavior prompted by a death wish. Such behavior to prove oneself not a coward bespeaks a strong internal conviction that one is a coward. When a person so beset by doubts adopts the heavy use of profanity and an exaggerated machismo persona, such behavior inevitably becomes cartoonish.

Patton wrote so much during his life not only because he believed himself destined for greatness but also because he had a rich interior life. Carlo D'Este relates in his biography a wonderful anecdote that sums up Patton's time at West Point. Years after Patton left West Point, his son, himself destined to become a distinguished general, donated his father's books to the academy library. On the last page of a textbook titled *Elements of Strategy*, Patton had scribbled the following notation: "End of last lesson in Engineering. Last lesson as Cadet, Thank God."

But that was only half the story. On the back cover he also left this directive:

"Qualities of a Great General"

1. Tactically aggressive (loves a fight)
2. Strength of character
3. Steadiness of purpose
4. Acceptance of responsibility
5. Energy
6. Good health and strength

George Patton
Cadet
U. S. M. A.
April 29, 1909

June 11, 1909—forty-three days after he wrote this and as one of 103 first classmen graduated that day—Patton sallied forth from West Point as a commissioned second lieutenant in the United States Army, determined to meet his destiny head-on. It would take another thirty-five years for that to happen, and he wasn't a patient man, which led to much unpleasantness and some serious lapses in judgment along the way. But as his cadet record shows, he was a young man possessed of the character and foresight to continue to prepare to meet his destiny when it did indeed present itself. So his every effort going forward was dedicated to precisely that task of preparation.

THREE

An Officer and a Gentleman

PATTON CHOSE THE cavalry as the branch of the army he would serve in. Following graduation he was instructed to report to Fort Sheridan outside Chicago. The peacetime army in those days was tiny, consisting merely of 84,971 men, of whom 4,299 were officers. These soldiers were scattered around the country in what were mainly small forts and garrisons, called derogatorily "hitching posts." Rarely did any of these posts hold more than a thousand men, thus approximately a single battalion. President Theodore Roosevelt had grander plans for the armed forces, but Congress and the American people saw no need for a large standing army or an outsized navy, and so refused to vote Roosevelt the funds to realize his plans. The military budget remained small, and the lion's share of it went to the navy to cover the cost of building and maintaining its larger ships.

This meant that the army was poorly paid and its accommodations, even for officers, were grim. Spartan was one thing, but conditions back then were downright squalid. When Patton arrived at Fort Sheridan in September 1909, he was assigned to bachelor quarters, where his third-floor room in a ramshackle building held only an iron bedstead and a mahogany desk. His first year as an officer was going to be an extension of his "rat" year at VMI and his two "plebe" years at West Point in terms of roughing it and being forced to learn on an accelerated schedule. But just as everything Patton did at VMI and at West Point played a part in his ultimate ambition to become an outstanding general, here at his first posting he fell into an early pattern that he would pursue throughout his career.

He found a mentor he admired, Captain Francis Cutler Marshall. Over time Marshall became the first of the officers Patton modeled himself after. Patton quickly noted how Captain Marshall handled himself, how he commanded men, and how he did everything with a sense of unbreachable dignity. Importantly, Marshall had combat experience as a veteran of the Sioux Wars of 1890–91 and the China Relief Expedition in 1900–01. As an added bonus, Captain Marshall had taught in the Department of Tactics for four of the five years Patton had spent at West Point. Tactics had always obsessed Patton; more than anything, he wanted to master the art of directing military forces arrayed on the field of battle. Marshall had deep knowledge in this area.

Within days of reporting to Fort Sheridan, Patton wrote

ecstatically in his letters of his good fortune in landing under Marshall's command. Marshall was a senior officer who led by example, a trait Patton revered and incorporated into his command style throughout his career. In a letter to Beatrice on March 23, 1910, Patton's first line was: "Capt. Marshall is a corker." As often occurred in his career, Patton was lucky to be tutored by so exemplary a commander.

Of course, the peacetime army could be boring, and in his letters Patton bemoaned the lack of war. He craved action, but none came his way. He did experience, however, his first maneuvers in a mock battle setting when Captain Marshall took his cavalry forces up into Wisconsin the following summer of 1910. When Marshall assigned Patton to lead a patrol and gave him additional responsibilities, Patton responded to the simulated war conditions with enthusiasm and acquitted himself well while leading the cavalry. This formative experience influenced him years later when he distinguished himself during the famous mock war maneuvers in Texas, Louisiana, and the Carolinas in the late thirties, prior to America's entry into World War II.

Two other events during the first year at Fort Sheridan are telling in light of later incidents that injured Patton's career. He lost his temper at a soldier he believed had been negligent in tethering a horse in the stables. Patton ordered him to rectify the situation by running back to the horse and tethering it properly. When the soldier started to walk rapidly, rather than to run, Patton exploded at him, snapping, "Run, damn you, run!" Within moments he thought better of this outburst, realizing quickly that he had lost his own dignity and at the same time had assailed the soldier's dignity by cursing him. Patton immediately gathered in front of him the soldier he had impugned and all the other troops working in the stable at the time. Then he apologized to the soldier publicly. This instantly endeared him to the men. It also marked the first time in his career that he would be obliged to issue a public apology. Unfortunately, it would be far from the last.

The males in the Patton family suffered from impulsiveness and often fell prey to impetuosity. As young men, Patton's father and his uncle Glassell foolishly became embroiled in a barroom dustup in Los Angeles. Biographer Stanley P. Hirshson, in his *General Patton: A Soldier's Life*, relates the tale of an early Patton military leader in the colonies, Colonel James Patton, who rode off impetuously with a posse during the French and Indian War to right a murderous outrage against settlers perpetrated by the Shawnees in western Pennsylvania. Colonel James Patton and his posse were never heard from again. The future World War II general may have been doubly cursed in this regard when one considers his grandfather Don Benito Wilson's volcanic temper and his refusal to carry a sidearm later in life for fear he'd use it rashly on the spur of the moment.

The other illuminating incident at Fort Sheridan drew on the Patton and Wilson capacity for stoicism. As with the first incident, at its conclusion it endeared Patton to his men. While giving a lesson in horsemanship, Patton was badly thrown by the horse. He immediately sprang to his feet and remounted, only to have the horse rear and topple over on him. As he pulled his leg clear to avoid having it trapped between the horse and the ground, the horse bucked his head backward and butted Patton, opening a deep gash on his forehead.

With blood streaming down his face, Patton mounted the horse a third time and completed the maneuver he had been engaged in demonstrating initially. Then he dismounted and—ignoring the blood still dripping down his face—conducted a class he was scheduled to teach in a nearby classroom. Not until the classroom lesson was completed did Patton retreat to the clinic and have the wound attended to.

These two incidents helped the Patton legend start to grow.

Patton's initial exposure to battle conditions in the Wisconsin woods spurred him to more closely read accounts of great military battles and to more avidly study military theorists like Clausewitz, von Moltke, Napoleon, and Sun-Tzu. Like a doctor engaged in a busy practice who nevertheless keeps up with the latest in medical knowledge and technology after graduation from medical school, Patton continued his military education throughout his career. About this time he started to read English and French military journals in order to keep up with the latest breakthroughs in weapons and technology as well as in strategic and tactical thinking. Beatrice, fluent in French, helped him translate the articles published in that language. Fairly soon he also started to write and publish articles on these subjects.

His first performance review from the esteemed Captain Marshall could not have been more laudatory had Patton written it himself. His commander praised his enthusiasm, discipline, loyalty, effectiveness with troop command, and capacity to learn. This set the precedent for a pattern that would be repeated within a few short years by General John J. Pershing, who looked upon Patton fondly and regarded him highly.

By early 1910, Patton had set his cap on making Beatrice his bride. But there were obstacles. Her father, Frederick, as an almost preternaturally successful rags-to-riches entrepreneur, naturally desired that his daughter marry well and securely. He did not feel that marrying a professional army officer, in light of the meager pay and the rough and sometimes wretched living conditions such a life imposed, fit that prescription for his daughter's welfare and happiness. Therefore, though he liked young Patton very much, he discouraged his daughter from marrying him.

This led to a clash of wills between two people, each equipped with determination that they would prevail over the other. Her father counseled young Beatrice about how foolish she was being, how unhappy she would become as a deprived army wife, how she would be forced to live beneath her standards and to consort with people beneath her class threshold. She countered that she did not care, that George Patton was the love of her life, the man she had to marry, the man she wanted as the father of her children. The clash between father and daughter grew worse, for each was as obstinate as the other. Beatrice retreated to her bedroom and went on a hunger strike. Late at night her sister Kay would surreptitiously raid the larder and sneak food into Beatrice's otherwise barricaded bedroom.

Patton then wrote a letter to Frederick Ayer assuring him that he would be devoted to Beatrice all his life, that he would see to it she was taken care of, that he had some means from his family, and that he and Beatrice would not live a demeaned and financially desperate life. Apparently this letter had some impact. Ayer reconsidered the situation, especially in light of the fact that in his daughter Beatrice he had met his match in a way he had not experienced before. Though he was a business titan who knew how to get his way and bend opponents to his will in commercial disputes, he eventually comprehended that in this domestic clash that happy outcome for him would not be the case. So he relented and wrote a warm, classy letter to Patton, and his daughter set a date and time for the gala wedding with Lieutenant Patton: Thursday, May 26, 1910, "at half after 3 o'clock," as the invitation read.

A lavish affair, the wedding was a great social event on Boston's North Shore, set on the grounds of Avalon, the expansive Ayer country estate in the posh enclave called Pride's Crossing. Ayer hired a special train to transport his Boston guests from North Station to the North Shore and arranged carriages upon arrival at the Beverly Farms station to carry them to nearby St. John's Episcopal Church.

Nuptial hymns augmented the ceremony, sung by the choirboys from St. Peter's Church in Beverly. No expense was spared, no detail overlooked. The traditional military touches were honored: the newlyweds departed the church under an arch formed by the crossed swords of four of Patton's classmates and one of his cousins while a large orchestra played first Mendelssohn's wedding march and then "The Star-Spangled Banner."

The guests included members of Boston's high society and Beatrice's mother's family in Minnesota, as well as friends and relatives of the Pattons from Washington DC, Virginia, and California. The Pattons themselves had come en masse from California by train, bringing with them carefully selected orange blossoms from Lake Vineyard, preserved in a box lined with wet cotton. These flowers adorned Beatrice's wedding dress, the same dress her mother had worn when she married Frederick Ayer a quarter century earlier. After the ceremony the carriages transported the guests back to Avalon for the reception, where a full orchestra awaited them on the terrace.

The next day Patton and his bride took the train from Boston to New York, where their bridal suite aboard the SS *Deutschland* awaited them at the pier. They sailed the following day for England and a marvelous honeymoon. It was Patton's first taste of foreign travel. After landing at Plymouth, the newlyweds toured Cornwell before going on to London. While in London, Patton availed himself of its splendid bookstores and bought a passel of military books, to which he added voluminously over the years; this initial London batch formed a cornerstone of the Patton collection later donated by his son to the West Point library. Patton could have had no idea then what a crucial role southern England would serve in his destiny thirty-four years later, when he functioned there as perhaps the most clever and deadly decoy in the entirety of World War II.

FOUR

The Olympian

TWO YEARS LATER, in the summer of 1912, Patton found himself back in Europe as an Olympian. In Stockholm, Sweden, he competed for the United States in the fifth olympiad of the modern era. This was a coup on two counts. It showed how fit, athletic, and daring Patton was; but it also showed how politically adept he could be, especially for a man of such legendary self-destructive tendencies when it came to being rash and impulsive. When he wanted to—and as a young officer he badly wanted to— he knew how to ingratiate himself with the powerful who could advance his career.

When it came to advancing his career, he never hesitated to exploit family connections and influence and he was severely disappointed that his father failed by a narrow margin to secure the Democratic nomination to run for senator from California in 1910. Had Patton Sr. secured the senate seat, as a ranking member of Congress's upper chamber he could then have done much to advance his son's military career, as Lieutenant Patton was only too aware.

When Patton returned to Fort Sheridan after his honeymoon in England, he applied himself as diligently as ever and carefully calculated his next move. He also laid the groundwork for it with aplomb. He taught himself to use the typewriter and threw himself headlong into reading and writing. Throughout his career he published many interesting articles on military strategy, tactics, and technological developments. He also formed a habit of writing intelligent memos to his superiors on possible policy improvements in regard to training and technology. Beatrice helped him enormously in this regard, always translating articles in French and helping him polish his English.

Patton was very aware he had acquitted himself well at Fort Sheridan under Captain Marshall, and he set a new goal of being assigned to Fort Myer, located across the Potomac from Washington DC, next to Arlington National Cemetery. As a Virginian, Patton knew the cemetery sat on ground once belonging to Robert E. Lee's Arlington estate. Even before Lee owned the land, it had belonged to George Washington, who bequeathed it to his stepson, whose granddaughter Lee had married. No facet of Fort Myer's prestige escaped Patton's notice.

Fort Myer was the foremost army showplace, a plum assignment that would bring Patton into close contact with high-ranking military and political leaders. He deftly used a family connection to pull off his scheme to be assigned there. Major Willie Horton was courting Beatrice's younger sister Kay at the time, and Horton had influence that he brought to bear to have Patton assigned to the 15th Cavalry in the late autumn of 1911. When Patton reported there a few weeks later on December 3, he had the platform from which to launch his rise to high rank and fame.

Fort Myer was famous for its equestrian excellence. Whenever ceremonial occasions in the nation's capital called for mounted cavalry, Fort Myer filled the bill. This held true for official state receptions for foreign dignitaries and for elaborate funerals for high-ranking government and military personages. The fort was also home to equestrian drills and shows, and it fielded the best polo team in the army—one of the best teams in the entire east. The army chief of staff and his team were headquartered there, as well as other upper-echelon army personnel. On one early morning ride, Patton met Secretary of War Henry L. Stimson, who enjoyed a daily ride as well. The two hit it off and became lifelong friends; this friendship would prove crucial for Patton's survival when he later became embroiled in one of the catastrophic miscues—the slapping incidents in Sicily in 1943—that threatened his career.

Patton had not been at Fort Myer long when he was summoned for an interview. His running prowess at West Point hadn't been for naught. The modern Olympics was to include an event for military officers, the revived Pentathlon. The modern version of this ancient five-part event would include a shooting contest with pistols on a 25-meter range; a swimming race of 300 meters; a 4,000-meter foot race; a fencing tournament; and a 5,000-meter steeplechase. Army officials knew of Patton's record-setting efforts as a track star at West Point and his having been a good fencer there as well. Obviously as a cavalry officer he could handle a horse; his marksmanship was a matter of record on his West Point transcripts; and he swam well as a cadet to boot, the result of all the swimming he had done in his teens at Catalina Island.

The army brass chose Patton to represent them in Stockholm. With his usual zeal he threw himself into training and was, according to his family, so maniacal about it that he was difficult to be around. He also went on a diet and eschewed alcohol and tobacco. In those days the Olympics had not yet become the large international event into which they eventually evolved. There were no national tryouts held a year in advance. Likely prospects were simply recruited to perform, as Patton had been, and prospects had only a little more than two months to prepare.

Patton was physically fit, relatively speaking, but he was not in training for such rigorously contested events. Nevertheless he hurled himself into training and went at it dawn to dusk—running, swimming, shooting, and fencing. On the way over to Europe on the steamship *Finland*, Beatrice, his parents, Aunt Nannie, and his sister Nita accompanied him. He trained on board every day, running two miles on deck at dawn with the cross-country team and swimming in an improvised twenty-by-eight-foot canvas tank on the fantail. While he swam in place in this tank, he was tethered to a rope that bit into his sides and left chafed runnels in his flesh.

For months he had been eating only raw steak and salad and

avoiding anything he considered fattening, like breads, puddings, potatoes, and other starches. He had especially pushed himself in running, at which he had grown rusty, and in swimming, which as a sport he did not like. He rightly considered running and swimming his two weakest points. At Fort Myer he had spent time on the pistol range, sharpening his already good eye, and he worked out on the base with fencing moves as well. His horsemanship, always excellent, took care of itself.

In Stockholm, however, he made a training mistake no athlete would make today, when knowledge of physiology is so much more sophisticated and training methods are a thousandfold more sophisticated: he did nothing the day before the event. The Pentathlon happened to commence on July 7, and the preceding night in Stockholm—due to its high latitude and the long days of the summer solstice—consisted of one brief hour of darkness. Because of this, the hyped-up Patton was unable to get much sleep.

The Modern Pentathlon began the next morning. It had drawn forty-two actual competitors, though sixty-eight had originally registered. Two other Americans, both civilians, had been slated to participate; but both had dropped out, leaving Patton as America's only representative. The Swedes, who had prepared their contingent for nine months, had eight entrants. The first event was the pistol competition. Each contestant shot two practice rounds. Patton's two warm-up rounds were tens, the highest score possible; but, of course, as practice rounds they didn't count. Inexplicably, when the actual rounds started, Patton did well in general but twice missed the target completely. He later stated: "This missing of the target, a thing I had done but once in all my practice, made me come out 21 of 42."

This mishap proved disastrous because Patton acquitted himself well in the other events and performed magnificently, under the circumstances, in two of them: fencing and running. In fencing, he was pitted against better-trained European officers, yet managed to finish third after two grueling days in which each contestant faced every other contestant. After the event he proudly remarked: "I was fortunate enough to give the French victor the only defeat he had."

Patton finished sixth in the swimming competition and third in the steeplechase, both admirable accomplishments. His strong finish in the steeplechase was especially impressive because he rode a borrowed Swedish cavalry horse unfamiliar to him. Only a gifted horseman could have performed under the circumstances as superbly as he did. His ride was judged as perfect, though he lost out to two Swedish officers by a narrow margin because their rides, also judged as perfect, were timed slightly faster.

Patton, however, made a near-fatal strategic mistake in the running contest. Before the race his trainer had given him some "hop," as the legal opium extract of the time was called. He went out fast in the 4,000-meter race but failed to pace himself. He entered the stadium in the lead with fifty meters on his nearest competitor but broke down and had to walk to the finish line. Two Swedes passed him before he reached it. He finished third but fainted after staggering across the finish line. For several hours thereafter he was in a coma. Because of the foolish use of "hop," he was actually in mortal danger while in the coma.

Patton's final overall standing was a fifth-place finish. No doubt he would have won a medal had it not been for the low score in pistol marksmanship, which ironically he considered to be one of his strong points. Most likely his lack of sleep the previous night and his nervousness in the competition's first event worked against him. Still, his family and his army superiors considered his showing a success, and it redounded to his credit.

As always Patton made the most of the opportunity presented him. His competitors were the kind of officers he admired: aristocratic, stalwart, dignified, unflappable, and uncomplaining even when a judgment call went against them in the games. Among them he made many friends. Having been the only fencer to best the French winner, Lieutenant Mas de la Tree, after the games Patton asked many of his former rivals and new friends who they considered the greatest fencing teacher in Europe. He learned it was the man acknowledged as the best swordsman in the French army, Adjutant M. Clery, who taught fencing at the French Cavalry School at Saumur.

Immediately Patton swung into action. While the Patton clan toured Europe, he convinced Beatrice to accompany him to Saumur, where he had hastily arranged for private fencing lessons with Adjutant Clery. For nearly two solid weeks, Patton benefited from private lessons on swordsmanship. Moreover, with Beatrice sitting beside him in the classroom, Patton audited courses in swordsmanship taught by Clery to the French Cavalry, noting his philosophy for teaching swordsmanship and the methods he employed. Beatrice, fluent in French, understood every word and each evening helped Patton transcribe what had been taught. Not only did Patton improve his own swordsmanship; he also learned the philosophy and techniques used by the best swordsmanship teacher in the world.

When Patton returned to the States in late August he reported back to Fort Myer while Beatrice went to Pride's Crossing to spend summer's end with her family. His notoriety now preceded him. He had received a glowing report on his efforts at the Olympics from the senior officer there, Colonel Frederick S. Foltz. In short order he was invited to a dinner with his new friend, Secretary of War Henry Stimson and the Army Chief of Staff, Major General Leonard Wood. That evening Patton recounted to these powerful men not only his Olympic experiences but also the experience he had undergone at Saumur with Adjutant Clery.

Thus Patton acquired another important admirer in General Wood, and for years to come Patton would send him memos suggesting improvements in drills, techniques, or maneuvers, especially as they related to the cavalry. Patton also served occasionally as an aide to Wood, and it was through this connection that Patton advised the Ordnance Department on the new cavalry sword. Based principally on the French model, the sword became known as the "Patton sword." Patton also received a laudatory and appreciative letter from General Wood when he completed a stint as a member of the War Department staff.

By careful lobbying, in 1913 Patton was assigned to Fort

Riley in Kansas. There he would attend the Mounted Service School beginning in the fall. During the preceding summer, however, he wrangled orders to once again attend Saumur and study further under Adjutant Clery. He did this and then went to Fort Riley, ready to study cavalry techniques more deeply. While at Fort Riley, he received good grades in all his subjects. Through proficiency at swordsmanship he emerged as an instructor and earned the official U.S. Army title of "Master of the Sword."

George S. Patton I, Virginia Military Institute, class of 1852, the general's grandfather who died heroically in the Civil War and influenced his grandson throughout his life.

George Smith Patton II, the general's father (standing), Virginia Military Institute, class of 1877.

Patton, age 7, with his mother, Ruth Wilson Patton, and his sister, Nita, 1892.

Patton, age 8, with his pet dog, sitting with his sister, Nita, in front of their childhood home, Lake Vineyard, 1893.

FIVE

Black Jack and Pancho

WHEN WORLD WAR I broke out in 1914, Patton tried to have himself assigned to duty assisting the French. His request was denied. General Wood, to whom he had appealed for help in landing the assignment, duly noted Patton's zeal in his official record. Wood told him he was too valuable a young officer to be risked in military service to a foreign nation. So Patton contented himself with service in the cavalry, where he continued to apply himself wholeheartedly and began to plot his next career move.

That turned out to be with Brigadier General John J. Pershing, known—not affectionately but derisively—as "Black Jack" because of his previous command of the 10th Cavalry Regiment, composed of African American soldiers. President Woodrow Wilson

51

called upon Pershing to lead an expedition into Mexico when Francisco "Pancho" Villa and his gang began launching deadly raids across the United States border in southwestern Texas and southern New Mexico. Although Patton was not officially under Pershing's command, he appealed to Pershing to take him along as part of the expeditionary force. At first Pershing turned him down, but then, when Patton went to see him personally, he relented and made Patton an aide, though one without official sanction. That is, Pershing did so on his own initiative.

Pershing subsequently became the chief influence on Patton as a military commander. Patton found in Pershing just the type of strict disciplinarian and participatory leader he himself longed to be. Pershing oversaw every aspect of his command and familiarized himself with every performance expectation he had for his troops. He believed in frequent on-site inspections and paid minute attention to every detail and nuance of troop drill and training. He led by example, and when the expeditionary force ventured into Mexico in search of Villa and his cohorts, Pershing bore every hardship imposed on his troops, including sleeping on the ground, and took many risks by leading them from the vanguard.

Even while Pershing did all of this, he insisted on proper dress and the best grooming his troops could manage under the circumstances. Despite primitive conditions and the tough terrain, Pershing did not relax discipline. No matter what came his way, Pershing shaved every single day. Second Lieutenant Patton sought to emulate Pershing in this and all other aspects of his military bearing and comportment. For the rest of his career, Patton's command style was based on Pershing's. Pershing went on to be the top commander of American troops in World War I, and his style when handling allies like the British and the French greatly impressed Patton, who would observe it closely as one of Pershing's staff officers. Later in life Patton privately and confidentially compared his friend Eisenhower to Pershing—to Eisenhower's detriment, especially when it came to handling allies.

Patton took dares in Mexico. He rode into dangerous terrain to deliver an important set of orders to one of Pershing's subordinates, and he led scouting parties in search of the Villa bandits. On May 14, 1916, Pershing placed Patton at the head of a foraging expedition. One of Patton's scouts had formerly ridden with Villa. When the scout recognized some members of a large group of men as followers of Villa, Patton had a hunch that General Julio Cardenas—one of Villa's most trusted colleagues and the head of Villa's personal bodyguards—might be hiding in a villa nearby in a place called San Miguelito, where Cardenas was known to have family and to have owned a hacienda.

Using three Dodge touring cars, Patton drove to the hacienda and surrounded it, blocking the exits with the cars and the troops that accompanied him. A bloody shootout ensued when three mounted riders attempted to flee the hacienda, shooting their way out of the patio and through one of the gates. A bloody Wild West–style gunfight erupted. In moments there were three dead Mexicans, including Cardenas, who had tried to feign surrender after being shot to the ground, only to come up shooting once again. He was then mortally shot.

Patton had his men strap the three corpses to the hoods of the Dodges. As they were about to leave the hacienda, a group of fifty riders appeared on the horizon, firing at the cars. Patton ordered his men to return fire and to accelerate the cars as fast as they could go away from the riders. This worked, although if one or more of the Mexican bullets had found its way to the gas tanks on one or all of the cars, Patton and his small band of troops may well have been history.

They reached Pershing's headquarters with the bodies still strapped to the hoods of the cars and presented them like trophies to their commander. Once again the Patton legend grew when the press picked up the story and ran it with a picture of Patton, called in the articles the "Bandit Killer." Beatrice, back at home in Pride's Crossing, visiting her family, read about her husband's exploits in one of the Boston newspapers. Once again, as with the Olympics, Patton received favorable public notices that redounded to his benefit with the army hierarchy. Pershing was clearly proud of his protégé and took to calling him "Bandit" in a joshing manner, despite Pershing not being known for having much of a sense of humor.

One significant element of the episode was Patton's early interest in motorcars. He had purchased one at an auto show six years earlier in Chicago, when he and Beatrice were first stationed at Fort Sheridan. As always, he was keenly interested in new technology, and he foresaw that self-propelled vehicles might have a future to play in military deployments as breakthroughs in weaponry. Now, in the wilds of Mexico, he had employed the first instance of motorized warfare for the U.S. Army by using the three Dodge sedans in a raid, much as horses had been used for centuries in cavalry raids.

Another use of technology interested him during the foray into Mexico with Pershing's expeditionary force. The fledgling 1st Aero Squadron assisted Pershing in his scouting and reconnaissance efforts by finding and flushing out the mountain hideouts of Villa and his men. Though these efforts were not truly successful, the early instance of using Curtiss JN-2 "Jennies" presaged their use a year later when the United States entered the Great War. The airplanes were primitive and quite unreliable, but Patton immediately saw the military potential of airpower, just as he envisioned the tanks to come with his first sightings of automobiles.

In the fall of 1916, Patton's father once again ran for the senate seat from California. Patton foresaw the benefits his father's victory could have for his own advancement in the army. But once again Patton Sr. was not elected, losing this time to the former governor of the state. But Patton's father's efforts helped to keep fellow Democrat Woodrow Wilson in the White House. When Wilson did not reciprocate by appointing Patton Sr. as secretary of war, his son was furious.

While Patton's father campaigned for the senate, Patton's sister had met and fallen in love with Patton's esteemed mentor, General Pershing, who reciprocated her feelings. They contemplated marriage, despite their twenty-seven-year age difference, yet it was not to be, for a simple reason: America's entry into the Great War.

SIX

Tank Commander

SERVING UNDER PERSHING gave Patton the great bene-fit of rapid advancement. Patton had taken the test for promotion to first lieutenant while stationed at Fort Bliss in the autumn of 1915, shortly before he transferred to Pershing's command. The actual promotion came on May 23, 1916, nine days after the heroic shootout at the Cardenas ranch. Officially Patton moved up a rung from the lowest grade of commissioned officer. His sub-sequent ascent was rapid.

When America entered the Great War, Pershing, who had just been promoted to major general, was quickly appointed to head the American Expeditionary Force sent to Europe. Although at the time Patton was slated to take on the duties of an instructor stateside, Pershing intervened on his behalf again and had him reassigned as one of his staff officers. Patton was delighted to leave with Pershing and his small advance unit for Liverpool on the liner *Baltic* on May 28, 1917, two months after President Wilson had induced Congress to declare war on Germany and the other Central Powers. As part of Pershing's inner circle, Patton found himself promoted to captain on May 15, 1917. This pleased him immensely.

What did not please him was finding himself as post adjutant at Pershing's headquarters at Chaumont, commanding such things as the 250-man headquarters company and the large motor pool. As he did at West Point when he was briefly cadet second corporal, Patton insisted on military courtesy, proper attire, and unwavering professional comportment. Everything under his supervision, man or machine, had to be in perfect order.

But this staff position was far from the combat responsibility Patton sought; battlefield distinction was the traditional springboard to rapid promotion, not administrative excellence. He had grown weary of what were essentially his housekeeping chores at headquarters when Colonel LeRoy Eltinge approached him about the possibility of becoming a tank officer. A "tank" was what the British had dubbed a new mechanized armored vehicle whose development had been pushed forward by Churchill and other British military visionaries. So far these machines had proved unreliable, dangerous, erratic, and only rarely effective. Yet their upside as a type of mechanized cavalry, spearheading troop thrusts backed by artillery attacks, especially in flanking maneuvers, was all too obvious to those with imagination. One such was Patton, and this is how he fell into the field of mobilized armored warfare that would make him famous and for which the school at Fort Knox would be named in his honor.

Patton wrote to Pershing and made his case for being reassigned to devote his time to the study of tanks. He cited his ability in French, his having attended school in France, his accuracy as a marksman, his experience as an instructor in swordsmanship, his status as a cavalryman who could envision the parallels between the uses of horses and self-propelled armored vehicles in combat tactics, and his having deployed three automobiles in his motorized attack against General Cardenas in Mexico, making him the only American to have acquired such mechanized combat experience. Pershing held him off on this question of tanks and countered with a choice. In view of Patton's imminent promotion to major, which would come through on January 23, 1918, did Patton wish to continue as a staff officer, or did he wish to command infantry? Immediately Patton opted for the combat assignment.

Now fate really knocked on the door. In the middle of October, Patton came down with jaundice and reported to the base hospital for treatment. He happened to be assigned the room next to Colonel Fox Connor, the man who legendarily mentored George C. Marshall and, even more closely, a young officer named Eisenhower, while they were both later stationed in Panama. Connor was a font of wisdom for the young officers who would form the cadre of military bigwigs who headed up the American effort in World War II. A soldier's soldier, a complete gentleman, a bold warrior, and a great analyst geopolitically and interpersonally,

Connor told Patton in the base hospital to ditch the tank business and attempt to become an infantry major. Patton agreed.

He changed his mind within twenty-four hours when Colonel Eltinge showed up bedside and informed Patton that on November 15, a few weeks in the offing, an American tank school would be set up at Langres. Eltinge asked if Patton would be interested in heading it up. He would. Patton was discharged from the hospital on November 3 and took command of the brand-new tank school. He had an immediate crisis of confidence and wondered how he should proceed. There were no precedents to follow that he knew of. He feared he had made a mistake and should have opted safely for infantry. But then he chastised himself that the important thing was that he would have a battlefield command as a major—whether in tanks or with infantry, it didn't really matter. Even better, in tanks he would be out from under the shadow of Pershing and would be able to make his own mark. Once again he felt his destiny would hang in the balance, and that was fine by him. He relished the opportunity to make it as his own man, and he really did like the promise the tank held as a futuristic weapon.

There were three other factors in favor of going with tanks. They were, first of all, new technology that nonetheless seemed to him to be a natural outgrowth of the equine cavalry, tactically speaking. Second, there would be hordes of infantry majors in this war but only one major in tanks, and he would be that major. Third, he did not really relish the prospect of being in the infantry for the same reason fighter pilots would later refer to the infantry as "mud puppies." The work of the infantry was down and dirty and lacked the glamour of the cavalry. The infantry slept on the ground, lived in tents or in the open air, totally roughed it, got filthy, and too often were maimed or killed. None of this appealed to Patton. The son and grandson of aristocratic cavalrymen, he saw himself as a cavalier in their mold; only he would trade in his charger for this newfangled motorized armored vehicle called a tank.

Because Patton went on to have such a spectacular record of achievement in World War II, his exploits in World War I are often overlooked or downplayed. Yet on an individual basis, they were equally outstanding. Moreover, they had long-range consequences for both him and the U.S. Army. Once he committed to heading up the tank school at Langres, he went at it with great energy and force. But first, as always, he prepared himself for the daunting task ahead by attending the French tank school at Compiegne, just as he had twice earlier attended Saumur to learn the latest techniques in swordsmanship practiced and taught there by the French master, Adjutant Clery. Though often accused of being impetuous and impulsive, Patton is not given enough credit for his willingness to learn and assess before moving forward, whether the task was mastering the rudiments of a new technology or winning a battle through superior reconnaissance.

Just as he had transposed techniques of swordsmanship taught at Saumur to his American classes in swordsmanship conducted at the Mounted Service School at Fort Riley, Patton now took notes on the circling "tautological approach" used by the French at their tank school and grafted this approach onto the teaching methods he employed at Langres with his first class, consisting of twenty-four Coast Artillery Corps officers. These men were chosen for their knowledge of artillery, since a tank was a form of mobile artillery. This was precisely the reason Patton had emphasized his top ranking in marksmanship when he first importuned Pershing to release him as a staff officer so he could take up the role of tank commander.

As could be expected given Patton's beliefs dating back to his cadet days at West Point and now reinforced by Pershing's example, he imposed discipline on his charges so that they would be exemplary soldiers first and tankers second. He especially made sure the accommodations for the tank-school students were comfortable and the food good. He wanted them to be highly motivated and set an example with his own behavior. Even as he ran the school and prepared the students to serve as America's first tank corps, he was careful to not overstep the boundaries and appear threatening to the traditional infantry; for that reason he always portrayed tanks as an added feature of the arsenal of weapons available to the infantry and not as the separate mobile armored force he believed they would quickly become.

When the opportunity presented itself for him to attend the twelve-week course at the Army General Staff College, also right there in Langres, he did so and thus cemented important future relationships with up-and-coming officers, none more up-and-coming than George C. Marshall and Adna R. Chaffee Jr. Patton attended the General Staff College during the day and then supervised the tanker school at night. He was hitting on all twelve cylinders and managing to pull off both assignments.

On August 20, Patton was attending a lecture at the General

Staff College when he was notified that Colonel Samuel D. Rockenbach wanted to see him right away. Colonel Rockenbach was in charge of the budding tank program for the U.S. Army and therefore Patton's immediate boss. The news Rockenbach imparted was music to Patton's ears. Pershing and Marshall Foch, the chief of the French General Staff, were organizing a concerted American attack on the St. Mihiel salient, a triangle-shaped wedge on the western front into which the Germans had penetrated deeply and that several prior attempts by the Allies had failed to push back. The attempts had taken a heavy toll in men and maté- riel, but now principally the American army was going to have a go at pushing the Germans back. Patton was thrilled they were going to use tanks in the attempt.

Four days later Patton announced the formation of the 304th Tank Brigade, also known as the 1st Tank Brigade, because that's what it really was. The tanks the Americans would use were the lighter and faster French tanks, not the more cumbersome and slower British tanks. The French delivered 250 Renault tanks to the Americans; Patton and his 304th took delivery of 144. Patton charted every tiny detail of their shipment and unloading at the railhead. He also did something he would do repeatedly later in World War II. He undertook a risky personal reconnaissance of the German lines he would be attacking with his tank corps and even walked the terrain of no-man's-land between the opposing trenches to test the ground for its ability to support his tanks. On this point he disagreed with his superior, Colonel Rockenbach, who thought the ground would not support tanks. Patton maintained from his personal inspection that the ground would support his tanks, provided the autumn rains held off and did not turn the entire plain into a quagmire of mud a foot or two thick.

A few months earlier, on April 3, Patton had received yet another battlefield promotion to lieutenant colonel. He was not about to fail in the U.S. Army's first tank attack. When Foch and Pershing and the other commanding officers made last-minute changes to the battle plans, Patton quickly adjusted and reworked his plan of battle. This was another signature Patton characteristic: his battle plans were always simple, direct, forceful, logical, and as plain and aggressive as he could make them. As always, he took care of every logistical detail, supervising the tanks' arrangement for battle and working out a system of communication and identification of the individual tanks according to the suites used in a deck of cards—hearts, spades, diamonds, and clubs—and assigning each tank within a tank platoon a proper designation, such as Five of Hearts or Four of Spades. Each tank platoon consisted of five tanks each.

This enormous attack, christened "the St. Mihiel Offensive," consisted of 550,000 American troops and 110,000 French troops. There were three separate tank forces in play during the offensive: three American heavy tank battalions using 150 British Mark Vs; a French regiment using the light Renault tanks; and Patton's 304th Tank Brigade also using the light Renaults. Foch and Pershing planned to assail the salient from three directions: first, directly from the west on the point of the triangle; second and third, from the north and from the south in a double flanking assault on the triangle's two exposed sides. The base of the triangle, its eastern side, formed the nonsalient German front from which the penetration had originated and to which the Allies intended to drive the Germans back.

A four-hour artillery barrage preceded the attack in the early morning of September 12. Patton and his tanks then moved forward with the infantry. At first Patton observed the action from a hill, but when problems developed, he moved down among the tanks and marched forward with them on foot, in the lead, with his insignia as a lieutenant colonel displayed on his uniform. Most officers make it a point to remove their insignia before going into battle because snipers naturally target them first if they can identify them. A holdup quickly developed when some of Patton's tanks bogged down in bad ground, but Patton unhesitatingly walked to them with a handful of officers. Refusing to crouch and duck, even though under heavy shell fire, he proceeded to help get the tanks moving forward again.

While still under heavy artillery fire, Patton continued forward and, as has been related many times, joined Brigadier General Douglas MacArthur on a knoll. The two stood talking while the artillery fire grew worse and came closer, neither young officer willing to leave until the other did. One well-placed German shell would have changed history, but fate smiled on both future legends, and they survived this reckless contest of willpower and nerve.

Patton left the knoll and moved forward again on foot as soon as he noticed German troops retreating. He immediately ordered his tanks forward. Eventually the tanks rolled into towns beyond the original points the prebattle plan had called for them to attain. The two commanders under Patton, Captains Compton and Brett, performed well. Compton's tanks rolled forward into the village of Essey. Brett's advance was also impressive, but it faltered from lack of gasoline. When Patton learned of the lack of fuel, he reacted instantly and typically. He marched to the rear echelon and saw to it personally that gasoline was quickly shipped forward to Brett's tanks.

All things considered, Patton's first tank attack was a success, and it proved to him that tanks had a big role to play in future combat. He was, however, reprimanded by Colonel Rockenbach for abandoning his command post, with its radio communications facility, and going into battle on foot leading his tanks. But Pershing understood. He wrote Patton a letter of congratulations on his success and on his outstanding leadership role in it. Rockenbach quickly dropped his censure of Patton for what he considered not only a too-reckless leadership style but an act of cutting him, the head of the chain of command, off from any communication. The experience of leading from the front further convinced Patton that his theory on heroism was correct: namely, that troops only exhibited heroism and could only be motivated to achieve heroism through the example set by their commander.

Rockenbach quickly deployed Patton and his tanks again. Only four tanks had been lost in the attack on the St. Mihiel salient, so Patton, as directed by Rockenbach, moved his force sixty miles north to a location just west of Verdun. Patton's tanks were there to support I Corps in its assault on the German lines in the

Meuse-Argonne Offensive. The Allies had intensely stepped up their attacks on the German front; in fact, within slightly more than six weeks the armistice would be declared, the Germans having sustained too many losses now that the American Expeditionary Force under Pershing was 1.3 million men strong and pressing the attack. Patton could sense the possibility that the war might end soon, and the prospect displeased him. He desperately wanted the war to last long enough for him to experience a great deal of combat.

Patton threw himself into the new assignment. Again demonstrating his belief in the paramount importance of good reconnaissance, he borrowed a French uniform even before the newly arriving Americans had officially relieved the French forces. Dressed as a French soldier, he went forward and surveyed the German lines, paying special attention to the terrain his tanks would have to drive over. Then, with his customary thoroughness and attention to every detail, he put together an aggressive battle plan.

After the usual heavy artillery barrage started in the wee hours of the morning, Patton got his tanks moving forward before dawn. But because of intense ground fog, he could not see the tanks from his observation post. With full knowledge that Rockenbach would again disapprove, Patton left the observation post with a small complement of officers and troops to see what was going on up ahead. Following the sounds of the battle, they moved forward to a point where they came upon five tanks completely bogged down in mud. As Patton watched this scene closely, he noticed the tanks would almost break free of the mud only to fall back when the soldiers working to free the tanks ran for cover each time they heard an incoming shell or a burst of machine-gun fire.

With his usual daring Patton hurried forward and seized command of the situation. He freed shovels strapped to the sides of the tanks and handed them out while commanding the men to stand their ground and dig, as he started to do. When one soldier proved reluctant to do so, Patton fixed that problem by striking him on his helmeted head with a shovel. The men followed Patton's example and dug straight through any shelling or machine-gun fire. Soon all five tanks drove off, advancing toward the German lines. Patton went along with them on foot, calling out to the soldiers present to follow him. This demonstrated vintage Patton battlefield philosophy: soldiers would be heroic if the leader was heroic.

The soldiers exhorted by Patton did follow, but soon they topped a small rise only to step into a hail of machine-gun fire, raking them all over. They dove for cover, including Patton. It was a transformative moment for Patton; he later wrote that he experienced a vision of his heroic antecedents hovering in a cloud above the German lines and looking down at him. He thought this was a sign that he, too, would now perish, yet another Patton cut down heroically in the midst of battle. Suddenly this vision infused him with calm, and he once again exhorted his men to follow. He and his orderly, Joe Angelo, started moving forward, but machine-gun fire rapidly felled the five other men with them. Angelo shouted this piece of intelligence to Patton, who shouted back for them to keep moving forward together anyway.

At that moment, a round ripped into Patton's left thigh and exited through his buttocks. He started to hemorrhage badly, and only Angelo's quick thinking and action saved his life. Angelo tore off parts of Patton's trousers and used the cloth to form a tourniquet. It stopped the hemorrhaging enough to allow Patton to order Angelo to run back to some approaching tanks and direct their guns against the German machine-gun nests. When a sergeant came by, Patton ordered him to contact Brett and tell him he was now in command since Patton was out of commission.

A medic appeared and properly bandaged Patton's wound. But Patton sent the medic on his way with instructions to tend to others who had been wounded. It took an hour for the German machine-gun fire to be subdued enough to permit a handful of Patton's men to come forward and carry him on a stretcher three kilometers to the rear, where an ambulance waited. Patton ordered the driver to take him immediately to 35th Division headquarters. There he made his post-action report and gave his gun and his money to Angelo to prevent their being stolen. Only then did he allow the driver to take him to Evacuation Hospital Number 11.

From the evacuation hospital Patton was quickly shifted to a rear echelon base hospital outside Dijon. This time Rockenbach was delighted with his performance and enthusiastically endorsed his immediate promotion to full colonel. Newspaper accounts gave the details of his heroism in remaining to command a battle from a shell hole even though he had suffered a severe and life-threatening wound.

Wounded on September 30, Patton was not discharged from the hospital until nearly a month later, on October 28. Exactly two weeks later, on the day he turned thirty-three, the formal armistice was signed, ending the war—just as he had feared. His wish to keep fighting, expressed in letters home, would be frustrated.

Patton's wound earned him a Purple Heart. He was awarded the Distinguished Service Cross for his heroic actions and the Distinguished Service Medal for his role in setting up the tank school and then in leading its graduates in battle. World War I had brought him distinction and tangible awards for heroism.

For Patton, however, it was not enough. He believed that his destiny still lay unachieved, that some bigger fate awaited him in life. He hoped it lurked in the future, but not too far off. His impatience couldn't tolerate a long wait. He had no way of knowing that he was embarking, with the outbreak of peace, on a long wait. It would be a period in his life marked by mental anguish, emotional frustration, domestic discord, dissolute behavior, and professional torment.

SEVEN

Between the Wars

PATTON NOW FACED two decades of restlessness. This is not to say he had nothing to do, but what he had to do did not satisfy his ambitions. World War I had filled Americans with a horror of the tribal wars to which Europeans seemed addicted. It was, moreover, a mechanized bloodletting on an unimaginable scale. A half century earlier, all of the European powers had sent high-ranking military observers to the United States to witness firsthand the mechanized horrors of modern warfare as initiated by the War between the States. The American Civil War had been the first war to use machine guns, railroads, ironclad ships, submarines, the telegraph, railroad-mounted artillery, and many other technological breakthroughs. These technological developments added to the slaughter of World War I, where Europe's Great

Powers lost whole generations of leaders. World War I added the lethal touch of chemical warfare in the form of mustard gas, which repelled peace-loving Americans. Isolationism set the tone for the two decades following the November 11, 1918, armistice.

Two years later, Republicans took back the White House from Woodrow Wilson and the Democrats. Warren G. Harding assumed the highest office in the land, with his campaign promise of a return to "normalcy," a neologism he or his backers coined. Military budgets were slashed. The standing U.S. Army was cut to the bone. From a wartime peak of some 4.5 million men at arms, the U.S. Army was reduced four years later to a bare minimum of 140,000. Almost every European nation during the 1920s and '30s had a larger army than the United States. In the mid-1930s, even the Polish army was larger. When the United States finally woke up to the reality that a massive conflict in Europe was again unavoidable, and that it might well spill over and threaten the democratic traditions and treasured freedoms of the American people, the U.S. military was in a big hole and faced a steep learning curve.

What this meant to professional soldiers like Patton and Eisenhower was that their careers would be stymied and their importance in the national scheme of priorities minimized. MacArthur, too, felt it, as did George C. Marshall. The entire military establishment of America was pushed aside. Congress slashed budgets and canceled appropriations. Americans entered an unrealistic cocoon.

Men like Patton who had won battlefield promotions in World War I had their ranks reverted to prewar conditions in what was once again called the "Regular Army," not the "National

Army." Patton's wartime rank of colonel was negated. That was three promotions lopped off—major surgery no matter how you look at it. This kind of demotion was common post-armistice. Patton naturally battled depression over it. He feared his father-in-law, Ayer, would be proved right; his military career would end not only in financial meagerness but in emotional pain and turmoil; and he would while his days away in a redundant, ignored, and disrespected profession, his one brush with heroism a distant memory.

One day after his demotion to captain, however, he was promoted again to major, which cheered him up a little. When assigned duty as a staff officer in Washington DC, though he loathed such a posting, he executed it as the professional he was. This assignment lasted only a brief period before he was assigned to Fort Meade in Maryland, a posting that would prove fateful. It would place him in close contact with the development of the tank for use in the U.S. Army, and he would befriend another young officer there named Eisenhower, who shared his enthusiasm for tanks.

Like one of his great heroes, Frederick the Great of Prussia, Patton was plagued all his life by bouts of depression. How he handled them is remarkable. He never allowed such bouts to short-circuit his sense of duty or those under or above him to witness them. Instead, through it all, he kept his eye on the ball; he kept his ultimate goal in sight, working toward it always, believing through the doldrums of the reduced and peacetime army that his destiny would yet beckon him and that he would fulfill it. In a funny way, fate did have its hand between his shoulder blades, gently nudging him on.

As a staff officer in Washington in the early part of 1919, he had been seconded to a committee investigating the potential of the tank. In that capacity he met and became good friends with an inventor who had previously served in the Ordnance Department with the army. This was J. Walter Christie of the Front Drive Motor Company of Hoboken, New Jersey. When Christie wasn't building race cars and driving them in competition, he built tanks. "Christie's M1919" was highly innovative. This tank could speed along at sixty mph, vault a seven-foot trench, and top a two-and-a-half-foot wall. When budget cuts forced the government developmental money coming to Christie to disappear, it is rumored that Patton privately supported his pioneering work with financial help. The army could not help because Congress vetoed the expenditure, though Christie's work was incorporated into many features of later tanks developed by the U.S. Army.

At Fort Meade, Patton and Eisenhower were so enchanted with the possibilities of the tank that they tore one down and rebuilt it by hand, learning every detail of its mechanical composition, much as championship auto racers are prone to do with the race cars they drive in competition. They wanted intimate knowledge of the machine's capabilities, especially when stressed to its limits. Patton and Eisenhower also drove the tanks themselves, learning their intricacies, just the way fighter pilots test the outside of the envelope so they will know what their plane could do and endure in a dogfight.

One day, tinkering mechanically with a tank, both Patton and Eisenhower were nearly decapitated when a cable snapped and whipped over their rapidly ducked heads. One other time a machine gun mounted on a tank jammed and almost shot them to death. For the accident-prone Patton, this was par for the course; for Eisenhower it was not. Democracy can thank its stars that they both survived their infatuation with early tank technology.

The National Defense Act of 1920 shattered their enthusiasm for the tank. It cut funding to the Tank Corps to the bone, rendering service in the Corps a career dead end. Both Eisenhower and Patton sought and obtained other postings. Patton returned to Fort Myer to head up the 3rd Squadron, 3rd Cavalry. All along he had continued his habit of publishing articles on military matters and putting together training memos and manuals. In 1923 he was back at Fort Riley, taking the Field Officers Course at its Cavalry School (the new name for the former Mounted Service School).

At the end of that year, Beatrice and his two daughters, born in 1911 and 1915, were back in Massachusetts at Avalon with the Ayers. On Christmas Eve, Beatrice gave birth to their son, George Smith Patton IV. Having a son pleased Patton enormously. It helped him deal with his depression over the skeleton state of the peacetime army and the eclipse of the tank program. Shrewdly, rather than brood and drift, he continued his education the following year at Fort Leavenworth in its Command and General Staff College, distinguishing himself by graduating in the top quarter of the 1924 class.

That educational feather in his cap made possible a transfer to the General Staff Corps in Boston, where he could be close to his family. It was also a prestigious posting, even though Patton had no aspirations to be a career staff officer. As ever, he wanted to command in the thick of battle. Staff officers were administrators. He was a warrior.

In 1925, Patton was assigned as a staff officer in Honolulu, at the famous Schofield Barracks. He was in charge of personnel as G-1 and of intelligence as G-2. Ever since Patton and Eisenhower had left Fort Meade and the Tank Corps behind them, they had conducted a lively correspondence. When Eisenhower also enrolled at the Command and General Staff College, Patton sent him his "Leavenworth notes." After Eisenhower graduated first in the class of 1925, Patton chided him that this was because of those excellent notes.

Beatrice and the children joined Patton in Hawaii. He did not enjoy the duties of a staff officer. He did, however, enjoy the weather and the opportunity it offered to hobnob with the island's high society and to play a great deal of polo with them, the closest approximation he could find to actual combat. The duties of G-3, commander of plans and training, were eventually added to his duties as G-1 and G-2. Before his career ended, Patton proved to be one of the best trainers of troops the U.S. Army ever had, but in Hawaii he was again too much of a martinet, perhaps because he was keenly frustrated with his lack of combat opportunities. At any rate, the responsibilities of G-3 were soon revoked.

The next thirteen years were not good for Patton. In 1927, his father's death threw him into a terrible tailspin. The following year his mother died. He channeled his personal challenges into his career and for the next few years shuttled between cavalry officer assignments and staff officer assignments. He made stops at the Office of the Chief of Cavalry in Washington DC and as head of the 3rd Cavalry back at Fort Myer. While stationed in the capital, he attended the Army War College and left as an honor graduate in June 1932, one of just two cavalry officers to earn that distinction. This distinction mattered—the War College is the highest institution of learning in the army, and only the top officers get to attend. Of those who do attend, only the top twenty-five graduates earn the "honor" designation upon graduation. Patton, fateful as ever, was number 25 in his class of 248.

In his capacity as commander of the 3rd Cavalry at Fort Myer, Patton had the distasteful duty of helping General MacArthur clear the Bonus Marchers from downtown Washington and from their "Hooverville" of tents and shanties on the Anacostia Flats, across the Potomac in Maryland. These Bonus Marchers, all World War I veterans, included Joe Angelo, the orderly from New York who had saved Patton's life at the battle of the Meuse-Argonne. The Bonus Marchers, all suffering the severe deprivations of the Great Depression, merely wanted the bonus promised to them as veterans, but that Congress had reneged on. The duty did not sit well with Patton, who esteemed soldiers above all others, but he did it anyway.

Two years later, in March 1934, he was elevated to lieutenant colonel, once again attaining his wartime rank. A year later he was again assigned to Hawaii as G-2, a position that did not thrill him. In his constant quest for high adventure, rather than take a ship, he sailed to Hawaii from California on his new yacht. Beatrice accompanied him on this dicey sail, but the kids followed, more prudently, by ship. He and Beatrice made it there safely in about a month, and he took up his duties as a staff officer. The children arrived soon thereafter.

Miserable in his new posting and in general beset with depression, he was a bear to live with at home. He started to drink too much and to womanize. In a lapse of his usual good manners, he did not bother to shield Beatrice from his philandering, inflicting unnecessary embarrassment and pain on her and on their two daughters. His son was too young to know what was going on. He even boasted of having an affair with his niece, Jane Gordon, the tall and very attractive daughter of Beatrice's older stepsister and a close companion of Patton's second daughter, Ruth Ellen, who was much compromised in the circumstances.

The only task Patton enjoyed in this second posting to Hawaii was purchasing the horses for the cavalry; for recreation he enjoyed playing lots of polo once again in the great weather. One such polo match, however, was not pleasant. In August 1935, during the Inter-Island Championship, while he was playing for the army team against a team of prominent Hawaiians from Oahu, Patton lost his composure and cursed out an important opponent, Walter Dillingham, a local business honcho and the most powerful non-military man on Oahu.

The commanding officer of the army team, Major General Hugh Drum, was seated front and center in the VIP box and heard the exchange. Immediately calling for the action to be suspended, Drum summoned Patton, dismissed him as captain of the army team, and instructed him to leave the field at once. At that moment Dillingham intervened and said he had never heard Patton use foul language (a near impossibility!) and that he was withdrawing his team in protest of Patton's dismissal.

Boxed in with no other choice to make, Drum relented, reinstated Patton, then left. Neither officer ever forgot the mutually embarrassing incident. Drum and Patton had known each other since their days on Pershing's staff on the American Expeditionary Force in France, and Drum had requested Patton in Hawaii as his G-2. There would be a follow-up to this incident a few years later. During the Carolina Maneuvers, Patton's forces defeated Drum's and—worse—took Drum prisoner.

Two years later, in 1937, Patton, Beatrice, and their young son sailed back on the family yacht to Los Angeles. The trip again took about a month. When they reached California, they sold the yacht and traveled home to Massachusetts for an extended leave of absence in the house they had bought there, called Green Meadows. While riding one day with Beatrice, her horse kicked Patton, and yet again he was injured in an accident, this time breaking his leg in two places. While recuperating he developed phlebitis and almost died of blood clots. Six months later he recovered enough to resume light duty.

The army physicians recommended that he be assigned teaching duties at the Cavalry School at Fort Riley. This was a good idea. Patton preferred teaching and training to staff officer duties. It also gave him time to fully recover from his injury. This, too, was a good thing. His next big assignment would be war games, and they could be taxing. Because war games were even closer to actual battle than polo, Patton was delighted to participate, though he had no inkling they would be his last tune-up before he sallied forth to meet his destiny.

EIGHT

War Games

BY SUMMER 1938, Patton's broken leg healed and he was fully restored to his energetic self. Equally important to him was his restoration—after twenty long years—to the rank of full colonel, first achieved at the end of World War I. After his short stint teaching cavalrymen at Fort Riley, he was placed in command of the 5th Cavalry Regiment at Fort Clark, Texas. There he reunited with Kenyon Joyce, the commander of Fort Clark, who had been Patton's boss at Fort Myer in 1934. In his evaluation report on Patton, Joyce had written that he believed Patton could be counted on "for great feats of leadership in war." Although Patton regularly received positive comments from his commanding officers in their evaluation reports, Joyce was Patton's only superior who ever wrote such an accurate prediction.

As ever, Patton drove his charges hard and instilled a culture of military propriety. He put them through war games and preached constantly that horses were obsolete. He was aggressive in the war games—attacking relentlessly, disdaining any semblance of a defensive stance, and continuously outflanking and enveloping his opponents (the "enemy"). He insisted that officers under him learn to do the same. Patton felt at home in this rough-and-tumble Texas border country, which reminded him of Southern California. Being back in the boisterous cavalry again made him feel very much alive. After the horrible domestic sieges he had put his family through, they, too, were happy at Fort Clark simply because he was happy.

Then, in December, Major General John Herr, chief of cavalry for the entire army, called to tell Patton he was badly needed back at Fort Myer in Arlington, with all its social commitments and its lavish and expensive entertainment obligations. Colonel Jonathan Wainwright could no longer handle the expenses of the Fort Myer posting, having no outside source of income. This same Wainwright would later gain fame as the general commanding the American troops who endured the Bataan Death March at the hands of their Japanese captors. Patton, known as probably the richest man in the army, could handle the expenses; hence, the summons to return to Fort Myer. Furious at this development, Patton blamed Beatrice and her money and excoriated her for it.

Stolidly, but with a good bit of residual anger, Patton reported back to Fort Myer. Once again, Beatrice and her Eastern establishment class and polish, in addition to her money, held sway on the high-society circuit of the nation's capital. Patton soon instituted horse shows and other entertainments at Fort Myer that found great favor with the general public and with the children of high-ranking military and government figures, and he was a success in the position. But, as always, he longed to be in the action at the sharp end and not in ballrooms and salons where the only punch was found in large cut-glass bowls.

Despite Patton's blaming his wife and her money for "ruining" his career, the move back to Fort Myer proved propitious. His old classmate from the Army General Staff College in Langres during World War I, George C. Marshall, had been appointed spring of 1939 as acting army chief of staff. Like Patton, Marshall lived at Fort Myer. While Marshall's on-post house—Quarters One, the traditional home of the army chief of staff—was being refurbished, Patton extended his home and hospitality to Marshall and his family, who accepted the offer.

A few months later, Germany invaded Poland and gave the first full demonstration of the power of *Blitzkrieg*. Patton smiled at the accuracy of his predictions about tanks and the future of warfare. Marshall was then permanently appointed army chief of staff and simultaneously promoted to full general. Patton polished Marshall's apple by purchasing a set of four silver stars he presented to Marshall as a congratulatory gift.

Because Marshall never tipped his mitt about anything, Patton had no way of knowing that Marshall was well aware of Patton's reputation as a trainer of troops, as a teacher and writer of theoretical articles, and as a tanker. He had Patton in line for promotion to brigadier general from colonel, but this could not be executed while Patton was still commanding a cavalry regiment, for that was a colonel's job. Though he kept Patton off balance about this, Marshall had earmarked him for command of an armored division or of a tank corps if America ended up back in a war.

Marshall considered Patton a character and remarked that he would "curse and then write a hymn." At the time, however, Patton was focused on one thing, and the outbreak of war in Europe made him all the more eager to get back on a battlefield.

In April and May 1940, Patton served as an umpire in the Third Army maneuvers in Louisiana. These maneuvers proved of seminal importance for the formation within the army of a separate armored force, autonomous and out from under the control of the powerful old-line chiefs of infantry, cavalry, and artillery. The maneuvers made clear once and for all the hopeless situation faced by cavalry when confronted with mechanized armor and tanks. Ironically, General Kenyon Joyce, Patton's old friend and former boss, commanded the overmatched and easily routed cavalry during these exercises.

When the maneuvers ended, a famous meeting took place in the basement of a high school in Alexandria, Louisiana, chaired by Adna Chaffee, the other now high-ranking friend whom Patton had met at the General Staff College in Langres during World War I. In the secret meeting these "basement conspirators" put together a post-action report laying out the case for a separate armored force. When the report landed on Marshall's desk, he agreed with its recommendations and created a freestanding tank force under General Chaffee.

Soon thereafter, Patton was back in Massachusetts at Green Meadows for the wedding of his second daughter, Ruth Ellen. While there, he read in the morning newspaper that he had been appointed to command one of the newly formed armored units, the 2nd Brigade of the 2nd Armored Division, headquartered at Fort Benning, Georgia. On July 26 he reported to Fort Benning and took command of his charges. He found them wanting and rapidly set about turning them into his kind of soldiers. As soon as he had shaped them up to his standards in dress and physical training, he turned his attention to schooling them as tankers. The U.S. Army has had few officers better at this throughout its history. The rapid transformation he achieved with these troops was remarkable. They were among the U.S. Army's first tankers.

At this time, unfortunately, Patton provoked problems on the home front with Beatrice, yet again. As a result, she went back to Green Meadows and left Patton to grouse and grumble around their quarters at Fort Benning. Contrite, he wrote her conciliatory letters, but she remained in Massachusetts, despite his apologies and entreaties to return. Her absence depressed Patton, but his mood spiked upward when he was promoted to brigadier general on October 2. Half a year later, in April 1941, his elevation to major general came through, and he was assigned as the permanent commanding general of the entire 2nd Armored Division.

Patton made the most of this enormous opportunity. He got carried away and designed a special uniform for tankers, cut from green gabardine and featuring white buttons slashed diagonally down the front of a tight white tunic. He wanted his men to look and feel elite. But the army rejected Patton's conception of what a tanker's uniform should be and elected to use a much plainer and more utilitarian uniform. Basically it consisted of standard khaki over which the tanker pulled on a pair of dungarees and a padded canvas jacket for warmth.

In the same vein as his grand scheme for a special tanker's uniform, Patton, with his aptitude for publicity and glory, staged a massive movement on public roads, a contingent of more than a thousand vehicles—tanks, half-tracks, and other self-propelled vehicles. It drove from Columbus, Georgia, home of Fort Benning, to Panama City in the Florida panhandle, and back. Along the way it received heavy media coverage, exactly as Patton had planned it would. He gave interviews and promoted the bright future of this innovative new division.

Stringing out so many vehicles in a straight line also taught Patton a valuable lesson. He feared this formation left men and vehicles susceptible to attacks from the air. To study this problem he took flying lessons—at age fifty-five—and bought a small, light plane. During exercises he took to doing flyovers and making mental notes of how to best avoid a unit being trapped in the open and strafed and bombed. By using his light plane this way, Patton conceived the idea of using light spotter planes for reconnaissance. From his close study of Civil War tactics employed by the Confederate cavalry, especially the horsemen under the command of General J. E. B. Stuart, a personal hero to Patton, he knew how important reconnaissance was, and it was always in the forefront of his mind. Four years later, his inspiration to use small spotter planes led to their successful employment by the U.S. Army from Normandy right on through to the Rhine and beyond.

Patton cast his fate irrevocably with tanks. Right after he was assigned to Fort Benning, he had been offered General Joyce's job as head of the entire cavalry for the U.S. Army. It was a job he had lusted after for years but nevertheless turned down now. He knew his destiny lay with mobile armored divisions. Between the wars he had read European strategists closely—whether German, French, or British—on the development and deployment of mobile armored weapons. He had studied tanks obsessively since the armistice, always using great politesse in discussing them, preserving his standing among the old guard in the horse cavalry, who looked askance at tanks and resented them. Patton went the opposite way, and after he received this new promotion, he read even more avidly about tanks and mobile armored warfare in general.

For years he had kept a close eye on the German general Heinz Guderian, the principal architect of *Blitzkrieg*. He diligently studied Guderian's published theories on the effective deployment of tanks. Before the outbreak of World War II, Patton was also aware of a little-known panzer general named Erwin Rommel, who had also written about the use of tanks in speedy attacks.

Now in his dreamed-about command of an armored division, Patton, according to Stanley P. Hirshson in his biography,

General Patton: A Soldier's Life, turned to a close reading of Austrian general Ludwig Ritter von Eimannsberger's *Mechanized Warfare*, published in English in 1935, a year after it appeared in German. The book emphasized that though tanks and other mobile armored vehicles could effectively serve in support of infantry, massed properly together they could also attack on their own and—music to Patton's cavalryman's ears—perform flanking, rear attack, and enveloping maneuvers with celerity and verve.

By 1941 it was clear that the United States would not be able to avoid inclusion in the spreading world war. The draft that had been started the year before had ballooned the U.S. Army. The skeleton army of 150,000 in the 1920s now stood at 1.5 million strong. To turn draftees into citizen soldiers took training. To prepare officers for combat conditions took practice. Hence, the army brass planned and executed three sets of preparatory war games. Patton escaped the fate of once again serving as an umpire, as he had the previous year, and instead was assigned command as a combatant. Next to the real thing, war games brought out his combat genius.

Patton knew the pressure was on him to prove the value of tanks to the skeptics. In the first war games, in Tennessee, he did just that. His training showed in every maneuver his tankers performed. He had been a great teacher and, in addressing his men before even these mock battles, his gift at exhortation came rushing to the fore. So, too, did his showmanship. He was his usual flamboyant self, leading from the front, wearing his full insignia of rank, disdaining any rear echelon command station. He was front and center.

In the first of the war games, he astonished his superiors by completing within nine hours the "objectives" he had been projected to achieve over a period of forty-eight hours. He was determined to make manifest to one and all the speed at which the U.S. Army could conduct armored mobile warfare. *Blitzkrieg* magic would not be limited to the *Wehrmacht*. He had taken step one in demonstrating that it could be adopted by the U.S. Army and even adapted to use at greater speed.

Four months later, in September, Patton more than doubled down his bet. In the intervening months he had driven his tankers hard—training, drilling, schooling, exhorting, and always teaching. He preached the greatness of the tank, dawn till dusk. The second series of war games, in Louisiana and East Texas, were the largest ever undertaken by the U.S. Army, involving four hundred thousand men. Importantly, Patton was assigned to fight for the Blue Army, under the command of Lieutenant General Walter Krueger, for whom he had respect; even better, Krueger's chief of staff was none other than Eisenhower. Unknown to Patton, Marshall and Eisenhower had deliberately put him in charge of the tankers because they knew his record in World War I and had charted his capabilities since then.

In this gigantic war game, Patton and his tankers stole the show. Pulling off a four-hundred-mile flanking move that enabled them to run half a circle around the opposing Red Army, they attacked it at Shreveport from behind. The Red Army had been assigned the defense of Shreveport; this did not make them look good. Patton's daring was breathtaking, so much so that there were cries from the opposition of "foul!" His defeated opponents claimed that Patton had violated the rules of engagement in sweeping so wide of the Red Army. Not only that, but Patton and his armored forces had traversed so much ground that his tanks had run out of gas. Patton had them refueled at filling stations, never denying allegations that he had paid for the gasoline out of his own wallet. The defeated Red Army commanders were angry and disgruntled. But most important, Marshall, Krueger, and Eisenhower were not. Marshall, as the ultimate authority, disallowed all claims of foul play against Patton, who emerged from the games as the visionary conqueror—the hero.

Patton was inordinately pleased. Only a few weeks later, in October and November, the army was back at it with a smaller war game staged in the Carolinas. Patton's tankers again proved they could accomplish speed and efficiency in warfare unknown in the U.S. Army till then. To spice his third triumph, Patton had the satisfaction of his men encircling and capturing the commander of the opposing mock army, General Hugh Drum, the very man who had embarrassed him six years earlier in Hawaii by stopping the polo match and trying to have him banished from the field because of ungentlemanly conduct and language.

But that minor triumph did not please Patton as much as the overarching fact that Chief of Staff Marshall had traveled from Washington to personally witness the proceedings. He came away even more impressed with Patton's performance. Typical of Patton throughout his career, when he captured glory in all three of these intense war games, he generously spread it around with praise and commendations for his officers and men.

A month later, the Japanese devastated Pearl Harbor early on Sunday morning, December 7, 1941, the day quickly pronounced by FDR as one that would live in "infamy." Five weeks later, on January 15, 1942, Marshall promoted Patton to sole command of the entire I Armored Corps. Naturally, Patton assumed that his World War I scenario would repeat itself. Now that America had finally entered the war, Patton thought he would be among the first assigned to combat overseas.

The forward-looking Marshall had other plans. He immediately ordered Patton to find a suitable site and establish a desert training camp for tankers. Taking to his small plane, Patton flew over deserts in the western states and finally found what he was looking for in eastern California near the town of Indio. Before making his final decision, Patton, like the cavalryman he was, rode over the vast desert stretch on horseback with a small team of staff officers. With nothing to recommend this 16,200-square-mile desert wasteland except temperatures as high as 130 degrees, sand, cacti, jackrabbits, bleached bones, snakes, and the occasional rock formation, it was perfect as a simulation of North Africa. Today that same installation, vastly improved, is home to the National Training Center and is no longer jokingly referred to as "Little Libya," as it was when Patton opened it.

Conditions were grim. There were no barracks. Everyone, including Patton, lived in tents. He disdained an elevated command post even here, in training. Instead of observing from above, he scurried about in a jeep, correcting and coaching his troops so they would learn how to fight with tanks to maximum effectiveness, even in the desert. That was by day. By night he wrote down the tactics and strategy the U.S. Army would employ in the coming desert tank warfare. And despite the harsh conditions and the withering heat, Patton made his men adhere to the tough physical conditioning regimen he always imposed. His conviction that this conditioning saved lives in combat never wavered. From April through July, Patton schooled and trained about sixty thousand men at Indio.

Then suddenly toward the end of July, he was recalled to Washington for a combat assignment. Though he could scarcely contain himself, Patton took time before he departed to sit down and write out a detailed report of his time at Indio that he titled "Lessons Learned." As with other initiatives he undertook, today such reports are standard U.S. Army procedure. Patton's battlefield glory has vastly overshadowed his prowess as an innovator when it came to teaching and training troops, but his legacy in these areas lives on.

When he arrived in Washington a few days later, Patton learned from Marshall that he was going overseas to command the Western Task Force. He would be in command of the first great battle initiative undertaken by the U.S. Army in World War II, code-named "Operation Torch." Its mission was the conquest of North Africa for the Allies.

Marshall, as he had planned for longer than Patton ever imagined, was going to pit Patton and his tankers against the vaunted Afrika Korps, which of late, under the brilliant leadership of Field Marshal Erwin Rommel, had been embarrassing the U.S. Army ignominiously.

Patton could scarcely wait.

NINE

Operation Torch

THE U.S. ARMY'S landings in Morocco went smoothly in the second week of November, and the resistance from the Vichy French was soon nullified. Patton and the Western Task Force had quickly fulfilled their goals. Patton's anticipation of a pitched battle had not developed. The Vichy French at first put up more-than-token resistance, but their effort quickly became somewhat halfhearted; they were not comfortable as allies of their historic enemy, the Germans. When they accepted Patton's terms, they readily cooperated with his plan for the continued governance of French Morocco and accepted their reduced role in it.

Army politics soon intervened, however. Patton had become uneasy after he undertook Operation Torch when Eisenhower installed General Mark Clark as his personal deputy commander for the operation. Despite the fact that Patton was eight years Clark's senior and far more experienced, Clark was nonetheless above him in the chain of command. Clark was something of a fair-haired boy for the U.S. Army at the time. After the initial success in Morocco, Clark had been appointed to lead the Fifth Army, instead of Patton. The Fifth Army under Clark would undertake the assault on the Italian mainland proper; it would be designated to land on and climb up the Italian boot. Hearing this, Patton feared he would be left behind and passed over for more combat.

Patton fell into a deep depression and confided to his diary his doubts about Clark as a commander. Patton believed the general could not lead men in battle. Patton also impugned Eisenhower's too-eager and acquiescent cooperation with the British. As a member of Pershing's staff in World War I, Patton had witnessed firsthand Pershing's take-charge behavior toward the Allies—especially the British, who had a reflexive, class-based elitist attitude of condescension toward the U.S. Army, its fighting men, and especially its officers. Patton, like Pershing, was having none of it. As he stewed and confided his discontent to his diary and his unhappiness to Beatrice in letters home, Patton received notice to prepare to host the Casablanca Conference between FDR and Churchill and their top military advisers.

As he seemingly could all his life—when his demons were not incapacitating him—Patton turned on the charm and was the perfect host for the two world leaders and their military entourages. His spit-and-polish headquarters and his sharp and efficient officers and troops made a good and lasting impression on everyone who attended the conference, including Churchill. Compliments on this score always drew the same response from Patton: he'd rather be leading his men in combat operations. It was his old disdain for staff work coming to the fore, as he feared he would miss the main action.

He quickly took heart, however. Roosevelt and Churchill decided at the conference that the deteriorating situation to the east had to be addressed and rectified quickly. That task would fall principally to the British under Montgomery, with the U.S. II Corps in an ancillary position. Being subordinate to the British vexed Patton, but the prospect of leading his troops and tanks in battle cheered him. What further cheered him was the news that, after Tunisia was fixed, the Allies intended to invade Sicily. Patton badly wanted to be part of this assault.

As a history buff, Patton was aware of all the great military figures who had successfully spearheaded assaults on Sicily. These included personal heroes of his, such as Hannibal, Scipio Africanus, and other legendary generals of the classical era in the Mediterranean Basin, when that was the entirety of the known world. To the Sicilians' dismay, ancient empires always jockeyed for position and suzerainty. Few other islands throughout history had been invaded and pillaged so many times. Patton yearned to add his name to the list of Sicily's conquerors. It perversely amused Patton that Churchill and his plan to attack "the soft underbelly" of Europe had won out over Marshall's and Eisenhower's plan to invade the Nazi's Fortress Europe solely from the west through Normandy.

For Patton, jumping ahead to Sicily was precipitous. The Afrika Korps in Tunisia, under Erwin Rommel, stood in the way.

Knocking the Vichy French for a loop was one thing. Taking on the *Wehrmacht* was an entirely different proposition. Februrary 14, 1943, one month after the Casablanca Conference concluded, Erwin Rommel sent the U.S. Army a strong message: the Afrika Korps was anything but a pushover. His forces routed and embarrassed the U.S. 1st Armored Division under Major General Orlando Ward at what became known as the battle of Kasserine Pass. The British quickly leaped to the conclusion that the Americans were hopeless. They even began referring to the Yanks as "our Italians," an allusion to the general ineffectiveness of the Germans' Italian allies when it came to combat.

Restless to be away from the action and stewing back in his headquarters at Casablanca, Patton took this blow to the prestige of the U.S. Army personally. And to intensify his feelings, his son-in-law, Lt. Colonel John Waters, the husband of his eldest daughter, Bea, was captured during the debacle at Kasserine when the experienced German panzer divisions, who had previously fought in France and in Russia, pincered the U.S. forces and enveloped many of them. There was consternation and drama within the Patton family as fear spread that Waters might have been killed. Patton was able to learn, to his relief, that his son-in-law was a POW and very much alive. Waters had been General Ward's executive officer.

While Patton was sulking in his tent at being left out of the fighting, Eisenhower telephoned and instructed him to leave the next day for field duty. Patton flew to Algiers where Eisenhower eagerly awaited his arrival at the airport. Wasting no time, Eisenhower told him that he was relieving Major General

Lloyd Fredendall of command of II Corps and replacing him with Patton. Eisenhower acknowledged that the task handed to Patton would be difficult. Fredendall had been a disaster as a combat commander. The troops were disorganized, demoralized, discouraged, and defeatist. Patton's job was to rehabilitate them. Time was short, and he had to do it fast—II Corps was scheduled for action in ten days' time. How Patton transformed the troops from a motley crew to an instrument of warfare in slightly more than a week has entered U.S. Army lore. As he had been in World War I, Patton was exhilarated at the prospect of fighting the Germans again.

Patton and Fredendall were opposites. The main thing Fredendall had done as commander of II Corps was to have the Army Corps of Engineers build him a heavily fortified underground headquarters in the side of a mountain thirty miles behind the front lines. There he stayed, like a woodchuck. He did not inspect or visit forward positions. From his subterranean headquarters, without viewing the terrain, he assigned positions to his units and directed his subordinates to station them there. The troops were incredibly sloppy, and rules were lax.

Patton changed everything. For example, breakfast in the mess hall was radically shortened and available only at dawn. No more breakfasts would be served at midmorning. Everyone would salute. Full dress uniforms would be worn. Officers would all wear ties. Fines were instituted, even for the smallest infractions. At first, grumbling and discontent were rife. Patton was loathed as he roared around, inspecting every troop installation in his specially equipped jeep with its flags and sirens, preceded by a motorcycle escort.

He drilled; he taught; he corrected. He conducted detailed exercises. He saw to it that the troops had the weapons they needed. The same thing held true for their food and clothing. He ensured that they had what they needed to fight well. And he addressed them as only he could. He told them they were going to fight gallantly under his command, and they were not going to be humiliated a second time. He emphasized, employing one of his standard lines—the profane delivery of which could vary in intensity depending on circumstances and who was present—that he did not want them to die for their country but to bestow that honor on the enemy. The grumbling and discontent soon subsided, replaced by esprit de corps.

On the strategic level, Patton resented a subsidiary role for his American forces in this upcoming clash with the Afrika Korps for control of Tunisia. He did not like being placed in a supportive role to protect the flank of the main British force under Montgomery. He did not appreciate the condescension inherent in the orders handed down to him by British general Sir Harold Alexander, who was in overall command of the entire operation. But he was determined to carry out the orders and conducted himself accordingly. Eisenhower sent General Omar Bradley to Patton as his personal representative. As politically astute as anyone when he was in full possession of his temper, Patton read this situation correctly and requested and received Eisenhower's permission to appoint Bradley as his deputy. Like Clark before him, Bradley was Eisenhower's spy, and Patton was fully aware of this, so he co-opted him.

Something then happened that elated Patton. On March 12, six days after taking over from Fredendall, he received his promotion to lieutenant general, something he had wanted since childhood.

When the attack started five days later, a division under Major General Terry Allen captured the village of Gafsa. This was uplifting news for Patton since Gafsa was the first assignment on the remit General Alexander had assigned his forces. Next Allen marched his tanks and troops toward Gabes, the second town on the list to be overtaken by Americans. Along the way, at El Guettar, they closed with advancing German and Italian units, and a fierce battle erupted. Twice, Allen and his men repulsed the attacking Axis forces, driving them back and wiping out thirty of their tanks. This was especially important because General Fredendall, after the embarrassment at Kasserine Pass, had painted a pessimistic portrait of American armor against what he characterized as vastly superior German tanks and weaponry. It was true that the Germans did have an edge in superior equipment, but Patton's men proved at El Guettar that this edge was not invincible.

The battle of El Guettar was heralded at home in all the newspapers, vanquishing the gloom that had spread over the home front after the mauling the Americans took at Kasserine. The *New York Times* cited Patton and his troops specifically for engaging German troops successfully on the flank and also praised the damage inflicted by the British Eighth Army at the main point of attack to the southeast at the Mareth redoubt.

The newspapers also described the trouble Patton's forces were having at the Maknassy Pass, where 1st Armored tanks and armored vehicles were bogged down by mud. These troops were under Major General Orlando Ward, nicknamed "Pinky" and very popular with his troops. Rommel had thrashed Ward earlier at Kasserine, and Patton believed he had no option now but to relieve him of command. He replaced him with Major General Ernie Harmon, who was very nearly as rough and profane as Patton. Ward's men resented the change, but Patton made it anyway, though he liked Ward and recommended him for a Silver Star. Patton then turned his full attention to taking Gabes to thwart Rommel's retreat from Mareth. Gabes was Rommel's port of exit, his escape hatch. But to Patton's acute frustration, his forces under Colonel Clarence C. Benson met heavy resistance, especially from German artillery, and were unable to close fast enough on the port.

In his frustration, Patton lashed out in a heated memo at the lack of air support from the British. This led to a contretemps when British air marshal Sir Arthur Coningham took umbrage and fired back a too strongly worded memo in rebuttal. Eisenhower's worst fears of the Allies engaging in counterproductive internecine squabbling and divisiveness were nearly realized. But the two angry generals ultimately reconciled in a face-to-face meeting at Patton's headquarters that began, according to their later accounts, with shouting and stares and ended in a pacific and enjoyable lunch. Eisenhower remained so upset over this blowup that he actually prepared a request to be sent to Washington that he be relieved of command for failing to control the Allied commanders. Luckily his chief staff officer and close friend, Major General Walter Bedell Smith, persuaded him to not send it.

In one last attempt to help Colonel Benson's troops and tanks break through against the heavy German resistance, Patton went to the front and found the tanks in the lead perched on the edge of a minefield. He recklessly drove his three staff vehicles into and through the minefield, leading the tanks across, only to find on the other side that the German forces had vanished in retreat, just as Rommel had swiftly withdrawn his forces overnight after inflicting the woodshed beating on Orlando Ward's troops and tanks at Kasserine.

In leading this charge across the minefield, Patton had disregarded Eisenhower's admonition to not take unnecessary chances in an effort to prove his courage. Seemingly Patton couldn't help it. He had to defy death, especially since only days before, a German aerial bombardment had killed his favorite aide, Captain Dick Jenson, the son of an old girlfriend from Pasadena whom Patton had dated in his bachelor days. His death deeply affected Patton, who wrote to Jenson's mother that he could not have been more shattered had Dick been his own son.

Patton wrote to Beatrice that his old horror of succumbing to his fear of death had returned strongly when he went to help Colonel Benson and his men, who were under heavy artillery bombardment. But, typically, he did not dwell long on this fear.

He had always known that death in combat was a possibility and had been reminded of the fact in a freak accident the morning of the initial Torch landings on November 8 when, as he stood on deck and prepared to leave the cruiser *Augusta* to go ashore via a small landing craft, Vichy French warships had opened fire and the *Augusta* returned fire.

During this exchange of naval fire, Patton had paused before climbing into the landing craft to strap on one of his trademark ivory-handled pistols. The pistol had inadvertently been left behind in his quarters on the ship and had moments before been retrieved for him by his orderly, Sergeant George Meeks. Just then the explosive muzzle blast from the *Augusta*'s rear turret blew the landing craft off its davits and shattered it into the sea in a thousand little pieces. Had Patton been in the craft, he would have died. Yet again, he believed that such luck only proved he had a larger destiny to fulfill.

The fact that the heavy action in North Africa would end in victory with the retreat of the Afrika Korps helped Patton avoid brooding on death. He had secured a substantial role in the mop-up operation for his II Corps, which the British had originally planned to exclude totally. Patton then relinquished command of II Corps to Omar Bradley and, as instructed, returned to his headquarters at Casablanca to focus his full attention on planning Operation Husky, the invasion of Sicily.

As Patton planned the next operation, he did not dwell on the missed opportunity represented by failing to seize the Port of Gabes. Nor did he dwell on his disappointment at learning that Rommel, who had been recalled to Berlin, had not been his opponent toward the end of this campaign. Had Patton been able to ram his tanks through to the sea and capture the Port of Gabes, he would have covered himself in glory for splitting Rommel's Afrika Korps from General von Arnim's Fifth Panzer Army and bagging both. The German rear guard resistance had proved too stout, however, and this opportunity was missed.

Yet Patton took heart. At El Guettar, an otherwise minor battle, the U.S. Army under his command had found its footing, claimed its true identity, and solidified its fighting prowess.

Patton, age 18, as a cadet at the Virginia Military Institute, 1903.

Cadet Adjutant Patton, age 23, U.S. Military Academy West Point, spring 1909.

Patton practicing the high hurdles for the 1912 Olympics.

Patton serving as an aide in Mexico with General Pershing on the Punitive Expedition in 1916.

Lieutenant General Patton wades ashore with rifleman at Gela, Sicily, on Sunday, July 11, 1943.

TEN

Triumph

AT CASABLANCA, PATTON worked with his staff on a battle plan for the invasion of Sicily. The Allied brass argued among themselves over that very plan, with the British unable to agree on a strategy even among themselves, let alone with the Americans. This squabble went on for three months until Montgomery cornered Eisenhower's chief of staff, Major General Walter Bedell Smith, in the lavatory at Eisenhower's headquarters and drew a very simple plan for him on a breath-smogged mirror. Montgomery's Eighth Army would land on the east side of the island's southeastern tip around Syracuse and head north; Patton's Seventh Army would land on the west side of the island's southeastern tip, around Gela, and proceed north. Montgomery would spearhead the main assault; Patton would protect his flank.

When Montgomery's plan was accepted, Patton did not relish being cast in a supporting role, but he kept his own counsel, glad to lead the entire Seventh Army and already visualizing a means by which he could not only upstage Montgomery, but also effectively steal the whole show. And that is what happened. Both armies invaded in the predawn hours of July 10, 1943. Montgomery's Eighth Army landed with relatively light resistance. The next day, the fighting intensified. Along the eastern coast road and inland as far as the main highway, which lay to the west of the eastern coastal road and ran roughly down the center of the island, the Germans and Italians fought gallantly. The Eighth Army had to scratch and claw for every mile advanced.

The amphibious landing was not so easy for Patton's Seventh Army as it had been for Montgomery's Eighth Army. High winds and rough seas disrupted the flow of the landing for the Americans. But after intense naval bombardment succeeded in subduing the German and Italian onshore artillery installations, the Seventh was able to get ashore and establish a beachhead at Gela. The next day, just as for the British to the east, the German and Italian resistance intensified. Amid the fierce fighting that day, Patton and his key aides left their quarters on the *Monrovia*, came ashore, and drove directly to Gela. Patton wanted to visit Lieutenant Colonel William Darby, his kind of officer, and his celebrated Rangers, the army's elite fighting force. Just as Patton arrived, the Germans and Italians unleashed a fierce counteroffensive.

Patton swung into action. He mixed with the troops and rallied and exhorted them, roaring encouragement and snapping off commands. At one point he helped load and fire mortar rounds.

At another point he mounted a rooftop and observed Italian tanks advancing across the plain north of town, headed straight for him. He shouted to a nearby naval officer, who was talking on a radio, to order the offshore naval guns to target the tanks. The cruiser *Boise* obliged and began knocking the tanks out of commission.

The most crucial contribution Patton made that day was a decision he had made months earlier. He had convinced Eisenhower to change the disposition of troops at Gela. Patton argued for, and won, the placement of Major General Terry Allen and his battle-hardened 1st Division, popularly known as the "Big Red One," as the main American force at Gela, replacing a unit composed mostly of less-experienced reservists. Bradley, commanding the II Corps, wrote in his memoirs that Patton's decision may have averted a disaster for his corps. Bradley believed that only the difficult General Allen and his combat-tested troops could have withstood the brutal German and Italian counteroffensive that day. Like Patton, Bradley did not like Allen, a hard drinker and a thorny warrior with whom Patton had an ambiguous friendship based on an intense and begrudging rivalry. That night back in his quarters aboard the *Monrovia*, Patton confided to his diary that he had really earned his pay that day and that throughout the intense fighting he had not been much scared.

Tragedy struck that very night, however, when an aerial formation carrying the 504th Regimental Combat Team of paratroopers was misidentified and shot down by naval artillery. The paratroopers had been on their way to reinforce the American troops forming the Gela bridgehead. Instead, sixty pilots and crewmen and eighty-one of the twenty-three hundred paratroopers perished. Eisenhower was furious, and mostly he blamed—perhaps unreasonably—Patton.

Over the next few days, Patton also incurred blame for one of his fiery speeches to the 45th Division, given days before the invasion. This was the division Patton had persuaded Eisenhower to replace in the vanguard at Gela with General Allen and the 1st Division. Patton had warned the troops of the 45th Division about the faked surrenders the German and Italian defenders on the island were using to bilk and kill Allied troops. In two separate incidents, a captain and a sergeant in the 45th ended up killing Italian civilians in what were investigated after the war as war crimes. Although Patton was eventually exonerated of any blame for these incidents, the defense lawyers for the indicted captain and sergeant tried to implicate him by claiming their clients were merely following orders laid down by their commander in his fiery speech.

These two drawbacks, the paratrooper tragedy and the possible war crimes incidents, seemed to further strain Eisenhower's relationship with Patton. In addition, Eisenhower rebuked Patton for going ashore at Gela on the second day of the invasion. He thought Patton had again taken unnecessary risks and should have remained at his command post on the *Monrovia*. Patton interpreted Eisenhower's displeasure as yet another instance of his accommodation of the British, for which Patton had faulted him in North Africa.

Patton concluded that he was on tenterhooks with his commander and wondered if he would be relieved soon. This explains why Patton did not protest when Montgomery successfully appealed to Alexander to alter the original plan of attack and widen his Eighth Army role by expanding its designated sphere of combat westward. By so doing Montgomery commandeered territory previously delegated to Patton's Seventh Army.

This shift in plans aided the Germans and their wizardry at defensive warfare by giving them a few more days to dig in along the main inland highway. Bradley and the II Corps could most likely have taken this road with expediency. By changing plans, the Canadians fighting under Montgomery were designated to take the road and, after the delay, only did so at greater cost in life and limb and matériel.

Despite being on a tentative basis with Eisenhower, Patton rightly perceived this shift in plans to be at his expense. It emboldened him to pursue the objective he had already envisioned, the means by which he would steal the show and demonstrate to the British that the U.S. Army was not a second-rate fighting force solely because its steep learning curve in North Africa had resulted in the debacle at Kasserine. Patton would prove that the British underrated the U.S. Army not only in its fighting ability but also in its ability to move with astonishing speed, especially under his command.

Patton resolved to beat Montgomery to the conquest of Messina.

Patton was determined to take the capital of Sicily, Palermo, situated on the northern coast about one hundred miles west of Messina, near Sicily's westernmost extremity. Taking Palermo had little strategic value, a fact Patton was well aware of. But he knew that taking it would generate positive publicity for him, for the Seventh Army, and for the U.S. Army in general. He saw this as compensation for having lost the inland road as an avenue to Messina, now that Montgomery had commandeered it and Alexander had rubberstamped this power grab.

Since Bradley and II Corps had now been denied the inland road, Patton ordered them to fight their way directly toward the northern coast road. Meanwhile, he requested permission from Alexander to take Agrigento and Porto Empidocle, two smaller adjacent towns on the south central coast due south of Palermo on the northern coast. Patton assigned the stouthearted and resilient Major General Lucian Truscott, like Ernie Harmon, another old cavalry hand, to take these two objectives. So Bradley and II Corps headed north on the vertical side of a right angle, while on the horizontal side Truscott headed due west with his provisional force assembled hastily by Patton expressly to capture the two small coastal towns of Agrigento and Porto Empidocle.

As soon as Patton set this dual-pronged attack in motion, Alexander reconsidered his earlier grant of permission for Patton to pursue this plan; instead he issued new orders expressly limiting Patton and Seventh Army's role to that of protecting Montgomery's western flank and his rear. This was altogether too much for Patton to abide. So on July 17, a week after the invasion began, he flew back to Alexander's headquarters in North Africa and formally protested his army's diminished role. Quickly realizing that he had offended his American allies, in compensation Alexander granted Patton a new remit: he was greenlighted to take Palermo.

Patton flew back to Sicily and set about doing exactly that. He cobbled together a Provisional Corps, placed it under the command of his number two, Major General Geoffrey Keyes, and assigned Truscott and his highly trained 3rd Division to spearhead the attack. Keyes and his troops covered one hundred miles of mountainous terrain in three days, mostly by marching at what was called the "Truscott trot," a near-jogging pace of five miles per hour. This is a mile every twelve minutes, nearly twice as fast as the army's standard of one mile every twenty minutes.

Palermo fell to Keyes on July 21, four days after he and his forces set out for it. As Patton expected, headlines around the world were large. Meanwhile, in order to accomplish this feat, Patton had turned a blind eye two days earlier when Alexander sent through revised orders rescinding permission for him to take Palermo. When Patton's adjutant initially received the new order rescinding the prior permission, the adjutant, knowing Patton's determination to capture the island's capital city, claimed the transmission was garbled, "misplaced" the order for a day, then requested retransmission, by which time, two days later, it was a moot point: Keyes and Truscott had taken the capital for Patton.

As he always did, Patton spread the credit around. When Keyes offered to delay marching into the city in triumph so that Patton could have the honor, Patton declined and told Keyes that since he had taken it, he should lead the march. Patton showed up two days later, after Keyes had enjoyed the limelight. There is, of course, some truth to the allegation by Patton's many enemies that he was a glory hound, a blowhard, and a showboat; but there is indisputable evidence, not solely with Keyes but throughout Patton's career, that he showered his subordinates and his troops with glory whenever they had won it.

The day before Patton entered Palermo, the famous incident with two mules on the bridge took place, a scene reenacted in the award-winning biopic starring George C. Scott as Patton. One of Patton's armored columns had encountered a delay on a stone bridge across a stream near the southern coast town of Licata. When Patton inspected the cause of the traffic jam personally, he came upon the two recalcitrant mules blocking the one-lane bridge. He looked up, realized the whole column was vulnerable to the *Luftwaffe*, snatched one of his ivory-handled pistols from its holster, and shot both mules in the head, killing them instantly. He then ordered the mules and the cart, to which they were still harnessed, tossed over the side of the bridge into the ravine below. The farmer who owned the mules protested, and Patton dispatched his concerns forthwith, furious that his ornery mules might have cost human lives and precious equipment had the column been strafed and bombed. The U.S. government, incidentally, compensated the farmer for the lost mules.

The following day Patton toured Palermo and instantly resolved to resume the race to Messina. Two days later he was called to a meeting with Alexander and Montgomery and persuaded Alexander to grant him permission, since he had ceded the main inland road to Montgomery, to pursue an attack along the northern coast road and along the inland road that ran parallel to it. Patton left this meeting determined to arrive in Messina first.

He went about it so ruthlessly that he clashed openly with his good friend Truscott and bickered with Bradley so intensely that their relationship was never the same again. Both Truscott and Bradley believed that, in his obsession to best Montgomery, Patton was not properly taking into consideration the danger in which he placed his troops with his aggressive attacks. They had a point. Patton tried three amphibious landings along the northern coast in an attempt to trap the Germans and Italians who were defending the road and to cut them off from their supply route and their headquarters communication. These landings were costly in terms of men and equipment lost, and were not highly effective in the end.

Yet Patton proved his point by taking Messina several hours ahead of Montgomery and the Eighth Army. Truscott and his 3rd Division troops marched into Messina and conquered the city by 10:00 p.m. on August 16, half a day before the British, who marched in early the morning of the seventeenth, the same day Patton climbed a hill outside the city and surveyed his prize, accompanied, of course, by the press.

In the aftermath of this campaign, just as in North Africa, Patton did not dwell on the setback that 40,000 German and 70,000 Italian troops had escaped across the Strait of Messina to the mainland, along with 10,000 vehicles and 47 tanks. Instead, he concentrated on what the U.S. Army had accomplished. It had captured or killed more than 100,000 enemy troops, had wrecked 265 tanks and 2,324 other vehicles, and had put out of commission 1,162 large artillery pieces. More importantly, it had dislodged an enemy thought invincible from a well-fortified mountain redoubt.

To Patton, the paramount accomplishment of the Seventh Army, which he told them directly, was that they had acquired immortal fame in taking Sicily and in the bargain destroyed the prestige of the enemy. Personally, he was incredibly elated to add his name to the list of Sicily's conquerors. But in the midst of all this triumph, his old problems with lack of self-possession and his inability to control his rage were about to cripple him more effectively than any enemy was ever able to do.

ELEVEN

The Slapping Debacle

AS PART OF Patton's leadership philosophy to be seen and heard by mingling among the troops, he included the obligation to visit the sick, the wounded, and the dying. Most religions label this responsibility under the heading of the corporal works of mercy. Patton believed it incumbent upon him to perform these works and did it more than most military leaders of his stature, despite the toll it took on him in depression, remorse, and guilt. He felt responsible for the welfare of his troops at all times. As Omar Bradley noted for the record, for all his snarl and bark and bluster, Patton was softhearted.

When he walked among the sick, the wounded, and the dying, he considered it a great honor to tell his men how brave they had been and how much he appreciated and admired them. He would have a cadre of his aides follow him through the hospital wards as he pinned medals on men who had earned them. His letters home to Beatrice reveal just how emotionally and physically taxing this obligation was for him. But he considered it his privilege, so he never shirked it.

That is the background to the world-famous slapping incidents, in which Patton slapped two battle-fatigued soldiers in Sicily in the waning days of its conquest by the Allies. There is no doubt that Patton should never have slapped a battle-fatigued soldier. It was a heinous act, and he is justifiably criticized for having perpetrated it—doubly so, because he did it not once, but twice. Today we know a lot more about battle fatigue and delayed stress syndrome and other devastating side effects of sustained exposure to dangerous or battlefield conditions. This was not the case in the summer of 1943. Still, common sense would have dictated that Patton show restraint, even granting his mistaken conviction that both men were malingerers.

Patton's lack of common sense does not excuse the inexcusable. The incidents, however, can be understood more fully by a grasp of Patton's own psychic demons. Patton had a lifelong struggle with an incapacitating fear that he might be a coward who would disgrace the legacy of his courageous forbears, especially his Civil War hero grandfather and that grandfather's brother, Patton's great-uncle Taz, both of whom perished from wounds in battle. We know that Patton often took reckless and gratuitous risks to prove he was not a coward. His inner demons would not grant him peace unless he exposed himself to death and lived to tell about it.

Before he came upon the two soldiers he slapped in Sicily, he had written to his wife of the stress and agony he had undergone in pinning medals on dying men during his evacuation hospital visits, some with gruesome injuries, one especially very hard for him because the top of the dying man's head had been blown completely off. Patton explained to Beatrice the difficulty he had in looking at this man.

On August 3, the day Patton slapped the first of the two soldiers, he received word that Eisenhower, despite rebuking him for recklessness, had awarded him the Distinguished Service Cross for his conspicuous heroism at Gela on July 11, the day after the landings when he had mingled among the troops, helped with the loading and firing of weapons, and called in seaborne artillery against the Italian tanks advancing on the town. Looking at mutilated and dying soldiers in evacuation hospitals made Patton question his worthiness for the award. He was not about to turn the award down, but he did not bear the pain and scars of the men who had landed in these hospital beds; nor had he paid the ultimate price many of them would shortly pay by losing their lives to their wounds.

The first soldier Patton slapped, Private Charles H. Kuhl, had no visible wounds or injuries. Fear and guilt gnawing at him, Patton jumped to conclusions and flew off the handle without understanding Kuhl's true medical situation. Significantly and perceptively, Kuhl had sympathy for Patton and later remarked he thought the general might be suffering from battle fatigue too.

The second incident, exactly a week later, involved another

private, Paul G. Bennett, who had been in the army for four years and had served with II Corps since March, under Patton and then under Bradley. When his buddy was wounded, Bennett suddenly became nervous, hypersensitive, and overly stressed. The medical officer had remanded him to the evacuation hospital despite his protests. He had wanted to stay with his platoon at the front. Though shaking hard with nerves, he had tried to sit at attention and answer all of Patton's questions and slurs.

It was again, as with Kuhl, a savage scene to witness. Patton in his own fragility saw "being yellow" or "a coward" as contagious, like leprosy, and truly believed that men like Kuhl and Bennett, though both had fought bravely, would infect all the other men with their sudden onset of nervous debilitation. Knowing himself well, having confided his fears to his wife and his diaries, Patton realized he was highly vulnerable to any such contagion. Hence, the overreaction and the tragic acting out on his part, the over-compensation erupting in the repulsive slaps.

Because the incidents came so close together—only a week apart—and since they rightfully appalled the medical personnel treating these two men and other victims of psychic incapacitation and battle fatigue, the medical officer, Colonel Donald E. Currier, forwarded a report on Patton's behavior to Bradley. Despite his animosity toward him, Bradley was loyal to Patton and filed the report in his safe. But a duplicate of the report went to Eisenhower, who immediately wrote a scathing letter to Patton, impugning his judgment, his lack of self-discipline, and questioning his ability to be of use going forward if he could not control himself under pressure any better than to do something as hideous as these two incidents. The letter devastated Patton. In compensation and in an attempt to rehabilitate himself, Patton at his own instigation made a round of apologies to the medical personnel and to Kuhl and Bennett, insisting that both men shake hands with him. He also addressed the assembled troops and apologized to them en masse.

That should have ended the whole matter, but it did not. Even though Eisenhower had asked the press corps around him to not publicize the incidents in light of Patton's crucial role to be played as a U.S. Army commander in the upcoming campaigns in Europe, word eventually leaked out to a muckraking columnist and radio show host named Drew Pearson, who made the incidents public on one of his Sunday shows in late November, three full months after they occurred.

A public uproar ensued, and despite all the publicity to that date building him up as a hero, Patton fell into widespread disfavor with the American public. Eisenhower contemplated canning him altogether in the swirl of this public outcry. When Eisenhower asked George C. Marshall what he should do, Marshall bounced the decision straight back to the *Supreme Commander*, European Theater. To Eisenhower's monumental credit, he did not abandon Patton, though he raked him over the coals. Eisenhower was nothing if not a man of enormous integrity, character, discernment, wisdom, and loyalty. He foresaw the good Patton would accomplish going forward and the lives he would spare through maximum effectiveness, on both sides of the conflict.

Eisenhower knew how much he needed Patton. He also knew how much the American people and the Allies in general needed Patton, flawed though he was. Eisenhower acted on his knowledge prudently. The American people and the Allies in general, however, did not know they needed Patton as Eisenhower knew it. Eisenhower knew just how much combat genius lay beneath the surface of Patton's obnoxious character flaws, and he wanted to avail himself of it as *supreme commander*.

Eisenhower would make Patton pay, through public humiliation and what amounted to a suspension, and then he would put him back in play. Even before the slapping incidents became worldwide headlines, Patton had watched in dismay as his Seventh Army was dismantled and reassigned piece by piece to General Mark Clark's Fifth Army for the struggle upward on the Italian boot. To drive the magnitude of his displeasure home to Patton, Eisenhower left him in Sicily with only a small garrison force of five thousand men under his command from what had been two hundred thousand when the Seventh Army was at full strength.

Fearing that his status in the doghouse might be permanent, Patton brooded. Eisenhower had other plans. Realizing only too well at this point what a loose cannon Patton could be, Eisenhower kept his own counsel and emphatically kept Patton in the dark about his plans. Like a grand master in chess, Eisenhower moved Patton all around the Mediterranean Basin, from North Africa to the Middle East to Egypt to the islands of Corsica and Malta. The trips were not clandestine, and Eisenhower knew that the Germans would track Patton's movements as they received publicity.

Humiliating as it was to him, Patton was being used as a decoy. Eisenhower wanted to keep the Germans guessing as to where the Allies would next concentrate their forces. Like the great strategist he was, Eisenhower wanted the Germans to keep their forces dispersed over a large area. Knowing the Germans had come to fear Patton more than any other Allied commander, and realizing they expected Patton to lead the Allied attack when it came, Eisenhower shuffled him to the max, stretching the German forces as he did so.

When serious planning for the cross-channel invasion began, Eisenhower moved Patton from the Mediterranean to the south of England, still as a decoy. Even in England Patton's movements were not clandestine but, on the contrary, were quite well promulgated to deliberately let the Germans know where he was. Eisenhower realized that Patton's forte was not administration and logistics. Therefore he used the quieter and more bureaucratic Bradley to actually supervise the planning of Operation Overlord, the cross-channel invasion, and to command its early stages.

While Eisenhower was moving him around the south of England in the run-up to the invasion, Patton committed yet another mistake. At Knutsford he addressed a group of women volunteers to the war effort and managed to tell them that the U.S. and the UK were destined to lead the postwar world along with their Russian allies. A reporter lurked in the room, even though Patton had been assured no press was present. When the reporter wrote up the story, no mention of the Russian role in governing the postwar world was included. This omission made Patton appear to have impugned an important ally.

The situation escalated quickly into yet another scandal because the press still sought to pillory Patton for the slapping incidents. Patton's mistake lay in accepting the speaking engagement in the first place; he should have been lying low. This latest enfant terrible lapse in judgment got Patton predictably into more hot water and yet again tried the patience and drew the wrath of the ever-understanding and infinitely loyal Eisenhower. To his enduring credit, Eisenhower persevered with his friend and nemesis yet again, showing that uncanny wisdom he seemed to possess in inexhaustible quantities, and continued to use Patton as a decoy, where he was most effective.

Patton had no interest in being a decoy, effective or otherwise; he was too anxiety ridden that the war would pass him by to think of anything else. That is not to say that postwar accounts of how obsessed the German high command was with Patton's whereabouts would not have amused him. As he brooded and fretted and feared that he was permanently eclipsed and passed over, he did not know that Eisenhower intended to turn him loose on the Continent just as soon as the early stages of the invasion were completed. Once the Allies had a secure beachhead, Eisenhower was going to unleash Patton to lead the breakout. There was no one better qualified to do just that; no one who drove relentlessly forward with one concept in mind: *attack, attack,* toujours *attack.*

Finally, a month after D-Day, on July 6, after eleven pained months in exile, his combat genius no longer eclipsed by disgrace, Patton flew to Normandy to take command of the Third Army.

TWELVE

Breakout

To HIS FRUSTRATION, when Patton reached Normandy and assumed command of his waiting Third Army, he had to bide his time yet again. The Allies had hit major trouble in Normandy. Montgomery was famously unable to break out from Caen, pinned down there by crack panzer divisions. Bradley, too, was unsuccessful in the difficult hedgerow country. His forces could not break out to the west of Saint-Lo, even though the First Army had launched a fierce offensive on July 3 aimed at doing just that. Among the Allied commanders, the fear of a World War I–style stalemate lingered at all times in the backs of their minds. Increasingly, the possibility of a costly stalemate loomed large after the initial success in June of establishing a bridgehead in Normandy. Bickering broke out among the Allied commanders about where and how maximum pressure should be applied to break through the German defenses.

Patton sat idle and observed the struggles his fellow Allied generals encountered. He had many ideas—most of them excellent—about how to succeed, but he kept them to himself, mostly because he still believed his status to be probationary. To some extent he was right. He had been Bradley's boss in Sicily, and yet now Bradley was his boss, so he was bending over backward not to appear insubordinate. With Eisenhower he was also tentative, believing correctly that Eisenhower had grown wary of his propensity to cause unnecessary flaps, politically, and unwanted disruption, militarily.

In mid-July, the British launched Operation Greenwood, designed to relieve Montgomery at Caen and break his forces out against the entrenched German panzer divisions arrayed against him. Greenwood called for heavy carpet-bombing southeast of Caen to blast a hole in the German defenses large enough to ram three armored divisions through. The goal was to seize the high ground of the Caen-Falaise Plain. The assault achieved this goal, but in a limited fashion; the Germans closed their defenses around the gap and remained in control of the battle. There was no breakout, only more prolonged and savage fighting in a strategic stalemate.

When the July 20 attempt to assassinate Hitler failed, a panicked Patton, fearing the war would soon reach a negotiated settlement, rushed into Bradley's command post and implored him to get the

Third Army into the fight. Bradley intended to, but only after he had tried a plan of his own devising. About a week later, Bradley launched a plan similar to Operation Greenwood, but on an even larger scale. He code-named his attack Cobra. After starting out shakily, even disastrously, it ultimately turned out to be one of the biggest strategic triumphs for the U.S. Army in the entire war; and for Bradley his greatest career moment. On two successive days, July 24 and 25, first the Ninth Air Force and then the Eighth Air Force dropped thirty-four hundred tons of bombs on the German lines ringing the town of Saint-Lo, which, after days of furious combat, had been captured by the First Army shortly before the saturation bombing commenced.

Unfortunately the aerial assault started horrendously— bombs fell short of their German targets and landed on forward American positions, killing 111 troops and wounding another 490. Among those killed was Lieutenant General Lesley J. McNair, in charge of all ground forces for Operation Cobra and the man most responsible for training the citizen soldiers who had become the battle-hardened GIs now pushing the Germans back in Europe and the Japanese back in the Pacific. He was also a friend of Patton's. Oblivious of any irony, Patton criticized McNair for being at the front with his troops and taking such an unwise risk.

For three days things did not look good for Operation Cobra. The German resistance appeared to hold. Then it suddenly dis-integrated. The difference was a hard charge by VII Corps under Major General "Lightning Joe" Collins. He sent two mobile armored columns into the target area slightly ahead of their scheduled time of deployment, and they met no resistance. The German defenses had broken down. Cobra thereby achieved its ultimate strategic goal: a breakthrough by the Americans, not a mere breakout.

On July 28, Bradley called Patton and told him to take command of VIII Corps under Major General Troy Middleton. Thus Patton was back in the war three days ahead of the noon August 1 target date for the Third Army to go operational. Patton immediately visited Middleton's headquarters, annexed VIII Corps to the Third Army, and set out to visit the front lines. When he discovered the 6th Armored Division held up on the near bank of a river, he disliked its commanding officers milling around studying a map. Wading into the river, despite visible Germans on the far bank, Patton tested its depth. Miraculously the Germans did not fire at him. Finding the river to be shallow, he walked back and ordered Major General Robert W. Grow, commanding officer of the 6th, to cross the river immediately or lose his job.

Shortly thereafter Patton encountered a battalion of the 90th Division digging in and ordered them to stop, instructing them to not fear a beaten enemy. He often equated digging a trench to digging one's grave; he despised digging in as the epitome of defensive warfare and preached against it vigorously. He had his army on the move and he intended to keep it that way.

Until now the American troops under Bradley had been bottled up in the Cotentin Peninsula, unable to break out. The key to the breakout was the capture of the two towns that dominated the peninsula's neck, Avranches and Pontaubault. On July 30, Patton's forces took Avranches; the following day they took Pontaubault. The two bridges spanning the See River in Avranches were still intact; so, too, was the single bridge in Pontaubault over the Selune River. For the first time since besting the German defenses on D-Day, the Americans had not just flexed but had actually snapped the German defenses, inducing a near-total collapse immediately following Patton's breakout from the twin towns of Avranches and Pontaubault.

It always suited Patton to leave the task of regrouping to the retreating enemy. With the Allies in control of Avranches and Pontaubault, the way was clear to the Brittany Peninsula to the west; and the path was open to the east and south across the plains of Normandy. Patton's Third Army pursued and vanquished the remnants of the beaten German Seventh Army in all three directions.

Over the next four weeks, Patton's name would appear in banner headlines around the world as he and his beloved Third Army racked up victory after victory, conquest upon conquest, throughout the month of August—probably the happiest span he enjoyed as a commander. He had gone from idle decoy to marauding avenger, rolling the *Wehrmacht* back to the border of France and Germany in the province of Lorraine. There, the party for Patton would temporarily end as the Allied victory in Normandy fostered a fallacious optimism. In winning so quickly and so thoroughly across Normandy, the Allied armies had outpaced their plans and their logistical capabilities.

★ ★ ★

Patton wanted to roll straight into Germany, correctly claiming that the Germans were scrambled and should be kept on the run. He claimed, probably with accuracy at first, that he could slash right through the Siegfried Line because the German defenses were in total disarray. The Allied commanders were squabbling, however, and Montgomery had devised a master plan to penetrate German soil through a concerted assault through eastern Holland. Code-named Operation Market Garden, this plan became as bad a defeat as the Allies suffered in Europe during the entire war.

Because supplies and forces were massed under Montgomery to the north, Patton was left to cool his heels in Lorraine. His tanks lacked gasoline and the armored vehicles could not move. The euphoria of the late-summer dash across France was supplanted for Patton by the dreary reality of being bogged down in the mud of Lorraine and subjected to its horrendous autumn and early winter weather, replete with soaking rains that turned the terrain into muddy quagmires. The thing Patton loathed the most was imposed upon him: an essentially defensive holding action. Old cavalrymen who are unhorsed are unhappy. The euphoria of the August rout turned into the boredom of an autumn slog as the Third Army pushed east, but slowly, hamstrung by lack of supplies—especially gasoline.

Patton's unsettled state had begun on September 1, when he heard on the radio that Eisenhower had promoted Montgomery to field marshal and characterized him as the greatest living soldier.

Annoyed by this, like the competitive soldier he was, Patton nevertheless flew that day to his command post and worked away at his desk on various administrative tasks. The thing that ate away at Patton was not so much Eisenhower's plaudits for Montgomery as it was Patton's very real conviction that the opportunity to keep charging east and surprising the disorganized Germans was being squandered.

It was not until the second week of September that the Third Army was resupplied. Patton immediately resumed his push to the east but knew, now that the Germans had been given a respite during which they could draw upon their phenomenal ability to wage defensive warfare, every inch of the Third Army's advance was going to be costly. He was right. The Siegfried Line had been reinforced and reorganized to withstand attack.

Although the Third Army managed to capture Nancy by the middle of September, the struggle to subdue the old fortified town of Metz would drag out for months. Metz was a town boasting a maze of forts, and though most were overwhelmed by the middle of November, one fort held out until shortly before Christmas, its three thousand defenders not surrendering until their food supply and any chance of prevailing finally ran out.

Interestingly, Patton's commanding opponent for the battle of Metz was Lieutenant General Hermann Balck, the head of Army Group G. Balck's troops had fought back ferociously from underground tunnels and rooms from which they had to be flushed out one by one. Acknowledging later that his troops were badly equipped and ragged, Balck mainly attributed their ability to hold out so long to tentative and inferior American leadership. This was the most cutting criticism ever leveled at Patton by any of the enemies he engaged in battle.

By the time the last Germans surrendered at Metz on December 13, Patton had been musing on intelligence reports about activities to the north. He was depressed by the fact that after the great run in August across France, the Third Army had advanced only a paltry forty miles since November 8. More than anyone else, he had been the one to turn Bradley's stratagem of Cobra from a successful tactical breakthrough into a sweeping and triumphant campaign across a vast swath of France right to the brink of the German border. Then he had endured the shortages of September and the horrors of the "October pause." Now on the edge of the holiday season, he planned to attack farther to the east, to shatter the Siegfried Line, cross the Rhine in high style, and march his victorious army into Frankfurt, one of the crossroads of Europe since its days as a principal market and festival town in the Middle Ages.

Yet he did not feel the charge he usually experienced on the eve of an assault. The intelligence reports he read from the north made him uneasy. He worried about Troy Middleton's VIII Corps, which, when it was part of the Third Army under Patton, had imposed an Allied victory on all of Brittany back in August. Now it had reverted to its original battle status as part of the First Army, situated to the north of Patton's Third Army. VIII Corps was sitting idle on the western border of Luxembourg, to the south and east of the small Belgian town of Bastogne.

With his preternatural feel for a battlefield and his uncanny ability to think in the shoes of his enemy, Patton sensed that the Germans were building up to the east of VIII Corps. Part of Patton's genius in detecting this possibility lay with his innate instincts as an old cavalry commander; characteristically, however, he had also availed himself of the latest wartime technology, and he insisted on being briefed each morning by the cryptanalysis made possible by Ultra, the extremely secret Allied code-breaking operation headquartered at Bletchley Park in England. Ultra was reporting no German-encoded traffic. Patton thought the silence was ominous.

Three days after the last German holdouts surrendered to Patton's Third Army at Metz, on December 16, Hitler mounted Operation Autumn Fog, known today in Germany as the Von Rundstedt Offensive. The brunt of the German attack would be aimed at General Middleton's VIII Corps in the heart of the Ardennes near the Belgian town of Bastogne.

Ten days later, on December 26, when divisions of the Third Army broke through the encircling German forces and relieved the American garrison at Bastogne, the greatest tactical feat in all of twentieth-century warfare was a *fait accompli*, and hard charging George S. Patton Jr. had kept his date with destiny.

Patton assesses the situation at Gela, Sicily, on July 11, 1943. Shortly thereafter he joined the front-line fighting when the Germans counterattacked. This drew a reprimand from Eisenhower.

A consummate trainer and motivator, Patton addresses the troops, Armagh, Northern Ireland, April 1, 1944.

THIRTEEN

The Bulge and Bastogne

THE VON RUNDSTEDT OFFENSIVE came to be known in the West as the Battle of the Bulge, though its official designation is the Campaign in the Ardennes. *Bulge* refers to the deep, bubblelike area of penetration—or *salient,* in military terms—the *Wehrmacht* thrust into the Allied front lines within the first few days of its attack. The last great German offensive of World War II, this fierce winter encounter became the greatest battle the United States Army ever fought and won. The cost in human life was staggering. The U.S. Army alone lost more than four hundred men per day throughout the battle's six-week duration. When it ended, the Americans had lost more than twenty-four thousand men. Casualty rates in individual U.S. Army units would routinely exceed 100 percent, with all troops in the unit replaced by fresh recruits because of death or incapacitating wounds. German losses were even greater. The *Wehrmacht* had taken an all-or-nothing gamble and meant to prosecute it to the bloody end.

At first, neither Eisenhower nor Bradley recognized the German counterattack for what it was. On December 16, winter conditions were so severe that they thought the reports of pre-dawn German artillery bombardment were intended merely as a calling card to let the Allies know the *Wehrmacht* was not simply huddled in bunkers, waiting to be overrun as soon as the spring thaw came. In former wars, when conditions grew this bad, armies retreated to winter quarters, as the Continental army at Valley Forge famously did in the Revolutionary War. So now, after the terrible fighting in the hedgerows of Normandy the preceding June, July, and August, followed by the breakout battles across the French countryside in September and October, and especially after the fierce fighting in the Hurtgen Forest and around Metz in November and December, it seemed logical to conclude that a winter lull would ensue. With armies on both sides of the front exhausted and suffering from the cold, snow, ice, and fog, the Allied leaders had assumed that the predawn German artillery burst was harassing fire, nothing major.

But it soon became clear to Eisenhower that much more was afoot than a bit of wake-up-call artillery fire. Reports started streaming into the Supreme Headquarters Allied Expeditionary Forces (SHAEF) that the Germans were on the march. Following the artillery bombardment, the massed troops behind the German lines moved forward shortly before daybreak. The Germans had decided to hold back their tanks until the infantry broke through. This proved to be a mistake. In the few instances where the Germans did allow tanks to escort the infantry, the American defenders were quickly overwhelmed and killed, wounded, or captured. Not so when there was no tank escort. Though surrounded and outnumbered, the American GIs dug in and proceeded—from scattered pockets of resistance, almost always with only small-arms firepower—to hold the crossroads that the *Wehrmacht* needed to take in order to advance its tanks, self-propelled 88s, armored personnel carriers, and even its outmoded horse-drawn artillery.

Hitler had been dismissive of the abilities of America's fighting men. He considered most of them to be semi-trained conscripts who would not put up much resistance when the going got rough. He was wrong. While absorbing frightening casualties and the wholesale loss of life, plus the largest mass surrender of U.S. Army troops at one time (7,500) in American history, the GIs fought gallantly, thwarting the German advance for what proved to be a crucial period of time. This delaying action was as heroic and crucial as any in the entire war.

Two elements of the Ardennes Offensive were especially lethal. First, Hitler had assembled and reinforced a spearheading armored regiment under the command of Lieutenant Colonel Jochen Peiper, a decorated veteran of many all-out battles on the eastern front. Peiper had earned two of Germany's highest military medals, the Iron Cross and the Knight's Cross. His armored unit, composed mostly of tanks, earned the nickname the "Blowtorch Battalion." The unit's modus operandi under Peiper's leadership was to storm a village at night under full speed with all cannons and guns blazing. Such a barrage ignited the thatched roofs of the buildings, burning them to the ground. Peiper and his 1st SS Panzer unit had subsequently seen heavy action in Italy before being deployed to France when the Allied invasion loomed.

Hitler handpicked Peiper to lead the special armored assault unit in the Ardennes because of his proven ability. Peiper's beefed-up and loaded unit was larger than a regiment, consisting of 22,000 men and 250 tanks anchored by his own notorious 1st SS Panzer Division. The tanks, many of them brand-new and sixty of them the monstrous Tiger class, had a phalanx of other mobile armored pieces accompanying them, as well as experienced infantry. Two companies of engineers accompanied him to help with bad roads and streams and to build bridges where necessary. Peiper's orders for the offensive were to lead this assault force through the Ardennes, roll on to the Meuse River, turn northwest, speed to Antwerp, and attack and capture it, splitting the Allied armies in two and depriving them of their main port for resupply.

The second lethal element Hitler had installed in his last-ditch counteroffensive was a unit led by the celebrated commando, Major Otto Skorzeny, another recipient of the Iron Cross and the Knight's Cross. Skorzeny led the German commando force that liberated Mussolini from his partisan captors and reinstalled him as the head of Italy's fascist government in July 1943. Skorzeny was to aid Peiper in his charge to Antwerp through stealth and deceit. He would lead the five hundred troops in the 150th Panzer Brigade who were trained in guerrilla warfare and sabotage.

Almost all of Skorzeny's troops were highly proficient in English, and planned to use their language skills during the offensive. Their plan was to wear captured American and British uniforms, often stripped from battlefield corpses. Dangling around their necks would be American and British dog tags acquired the same way. Their armored vehicles would consist of twenty captured Sherman tanks and thirty two-and-a-half-ton trucks. They had also captured American and British weapons, including sidearms, rifles, and machine guns. Their disguises were complete.

Once Peiper's armored task force and infantry broke through the Allied lines, Skorzeny's troops were to have two objectives. Half of them would race for the Meuse to seize and hold the bridges for Peiper and his tanks and troops. The other half would sow havoc and panic behind the Allied lines. Skorzeny knew that in battle, whenever the front line breaks, the rear-echelon troops, feeling vulnerable and exposed, often panic and flee. He and his troops were determined to speed up and intensify this natural reaction.

Their entire commando operation was a devilishly clever ruse, and in the first few days of the battle, it proved effective. Their success led wary Americans, when suspecting German men among their troops, to give pop quizzes like, "What Yankee was nicknamed the Iron Horse?" or "What team was called the Gas House Gang?" or similar tricky questions designed to trip them up. This happened even in the heat of battle.

Peiper and Skorzeny reported to another of Hitler's favorite officers, General Sepp Dietrich, who had command of the entire

Sixth Panzer Army. The overall objective of the Sixth Army, positioned at the northernmost point of the German attack, was to smash through the American lines between Aachen to the north and Shnee Eifel to the south. Then it was to seize the bridges across the Meuse on either side of Liege and hold them to enable Peiper's passage westward.

Bastogne is a small Belgian town in the Ardennes, a forested region near the German border. When the Germans launched their surprise counteroffensive, they trapped the American troops defending the town so quickly and thoroughly that Eisenhower rushed the 101st Airborne to save them. The "Screaming Eagles" division had been resting and reconstituting itself behind the lines, taking in many replacements. The 101st had seen heavy fighting and suffered many casualties throughout the summer months from D-Day through the Normandy campaign and on across France to the edge of the German border. They were exhausted and had been sent to the rear echelon for rest and recuperation.

Eisenhower had no choice but to call them up. He also called up the 82nd Airborne, the "All American" division, which, like the 101st, had been resting and integrating many replacement troops because it, too, had fought since D-Day and had suffered many casualties. Eisenhower had no choice but to move both crack paratrooper divisions forward in the Ardennes, assigning the 101st to the defense of Bastogne and the 82nd to the American front north of Bastogne, where the defenses were collapsing.

The *Wehrmacht* overwhelmed the American troops, causing them to panic and retreat in the most disorderly fashion for the U.S. Army since the rout at First Manassas in 1861. Some, however, refused to panic and run. These heroic American troops dug in and thwarted the German advance, brilliantly and gallantly holding key crossroads until the paratroopers and other reinforcements arrived. Many of these brave men died, and many others were either severely wounded or captured, sometimes both.

Skorzeny and his commandos succeeded in escalating the panic that overtook many American troops as the front disintegrated in the first three days. The German commands approached American troops disguised as Allied forces, usually American, and gunned them down; they changed road signs and caused chaos with American military traffic; they infiltrated American positions and spread rumors; and they sabotaged American vehicles and weapons. Skorzeny and his commandos had made an auspicious start.

Peiper's large armored forces were moving, too, but not as quickly as they had planned. Peiper had to wait almost a full day to get under way because the German paratroopers charged with forging a breach in the American lines could not do it. Hitler had underestimated the fighting capability of the ordinary American troops when he drew up his plans. Then, as Eisenhower and Bradley had counted on when they deemed a winter attack through the Ardennes not feasible, the roads gave Peiper and his heavy armor trouble when they did get started. After the war, Peiper stated that the roads they had to use were better suited to bicycles than armored behemoths like Panther and Tiger tanks, especially since the snow, hail, and icy rain had formed deep mud on most of the roads. Peiper and his tanks finally managed to move forward shortly before dawn on December 17. Besides the lousy road conditions, they were hampered when they ran into a column of American artillery observers, even though Peiper and his tanks made quick work of them.

December 17 was the day Peiper and his men allegedly perpetrated the Malmedy Massacre, in which American troops who had been prisoners were gunned down near the small town of Malmedy. Some of Skorzeny's commandos moved among the fallen Americans in the field where they were slaughtered and asked in English if anyone needed help. Those who answered were shot in the head. This incident formed the basis for war crimes trials after the war. Peiper had left a trail of war crimes on the eastern front for which the Russians, after the war, sentenced him in absentia to hanging. On his push toward the Meuse this time, he was also accused of killing Belgian civilians. After the war he was accused of having issued an order to his troops that no mercy was to be shown to either combatant or civilian and no prisoners taken. During postwar trials he denied this.

He made progress on December 17 and 18, as did Dietrich's entire Sixth Army. So, too, did the other German armies on the attack, the Fifth and the Seventh. In sheer numbers they overwhelmed the Americans, enjoying in some instances a ten-to-one advantage. In the preceding two months, Hitler had nearly tripled the number of troops assigned to the western front. To be on the offensive again was a tonic for the *Wehrmacht*, evoking memories of the wild assault through the Low Countries, Luxembourg, and France in May 1940.

When the Germans attacked through the Ardennes, General Patton and his Third Army were arrayed to the south, ranging about sixty to one hundred miles from Bastogne. Patton and his army had been fighting and gaining territory ever since July when they landed in Normandy and went on the offensive with Bradley and his First and Twelfth Armies after the breakout at Saint-Lo. So successful had Patton and his Third Army been that they were now only about twenty miles from the Siegfried Line, where Germany's fabled defenses were mounted. Patton, convinced that he and his army could breach the Siegfried Line, had been imploring Eisenhower to send him more fuel for his tanks. Eisenhower refused, sticking instead to his "broad front" strategy. He considered Patton too far into the vanguard in relation to the armies attacking in the north. He wanted Patton to hold up and not overexpose his forces to counterattack through too deep a penetration into enemy territory, where they could be assailed from all sides.

After the war Patton would state that, instead of going into Eisenhower's holding pattern, he advocated a pincer movement that would trap the majority of the *Wehrmacht* in its snare. Under this plan, he and the Third Army would attack from the south while Montgomery and the combined British and American armies under his command would attack from the north. They would have met in the middle. It would have been a simple enveloping maneuver, and Patton, a famously devout student of military history, cited many historical precedents illustrating its effectiveness. Patton had come to his plan after studying maps of the current battlefield disposition of forces. Startling in its simplicity, his grand plan might well have worked, but it was quickly rendered moot as a proposition when the Germans beat the Allies to the punch and launched their counteroffensive.

Hitler had assumed that Eisenhower would not grasp the scope of the German counteroffensive quickly, and that once he did, he would need to consult with Roosevelt and Churchill in order to reshuffle his priorities away from the offensives north and south of the Ardennes, in the north under Montgomery, in the south under Bradley. Bradley's offensive featured Patton and his Third Army, now quite far into the vanguard at Metz. Hitler calculated that by the time Eisenhower shifted his forces from the north and south offensives to a defensive action in the Ardennes, Germany's Sixth Army would have crossed the Meuse and turned sharply north toward Antwerp with too much momentum for the Allies to stop them.

Hitler miscalculated Eisenhower on three counts: his autonomy, his tactical abilities, and his logistical mastery. Although Bradley stuck to his initial analysis that the German artillery barrage on December 16 was merely a "spoiling attack" intended as a diversion, Eisenhower saw it for what it was and took remedial action. He told Bradley it was not a mere counterattack but a concerted counteroffensive. He ordered an armored division each to station itself at the north and south points of the German penetration, thereby restricting the width of the German salient, the bulge, preventing its spread.

Then, on December 17, he apologized in a phone call to his boss back in Washington, General George C. Marshall, for the breakdown in Allied intelligence that had led to the German attack coming as a complete surprise. That was the last time Eisenhower addressed his attention to the past. Instead he huddled with his general staff and went over all dispositions of troops on the maps and in the rear echelon. When he had assessed the situation thoroughly for two days and had his mind clear, he instructed Bradley to call Patton and tell him to meet with them the next morning, on December 19, in Verdun.

Verdun was a significant choice for this crucial meeting. It was at Verdun that perhaps the greatest and bloodiest battle of World War I was fought. Ever since then visitors had been discomfited by its extensive ossuary, an entire building filled with the bones of soldiers who had died there. Because of the carnage it witnessed in the Great War, Verdun is such a sacrosanct venue that it is still forbidden to blow a car horn there out of respect for the fallen.

During the same three days that Eisenhower assessed his strengths and options, Patton, more than a hundred miles away in his Third Army headquarters at Metz, was doing the same thing. Patton had a preternatural ability to assess a battlefield, to anticipate his opponent's strategy and tactics, and to take action that preempted the enemy's initiative and neutralized any chance at success the battle plan might have had. Significantly, since December 12, Patton had been speculating about a German attack north of his Third Army's southern penetration, above his northern flank. He had even discussed contingent action with his key staff officers in the event this possibility materialized, and together they had drawn up provisional plans.

On the night of December 16, Patton received a call from General Allen, chief of staff of the Twelfth Army Group. Allen was positioned with the First Army in the north. He requested that Patton's 10th Armored Division be attached to the VIII Corps of the First Army to help repel a strong German attack in the Ardennes. Patton knew immediately that his hunch about a German attack had been right. But, as he admitted in his posthumous memoir, *War As I Knew It*, he did not yet realize the seriousness of the German counteroffensive.

On December 17, information about events to the north filtered in to Patton's headquarters. At that point, however, he still held to his plan to have the Third Army attack the Siegfried Line. This all changed a day later. Bradley called at ten-thirty the morning of December 18 and asked Patton to collect his three top staff officers and come with them to his headquarters in Luxembourg. When Patton got there, Bradley showed him that the German penetration was much deeper than Patton realized. He then asked Patton what he could do about it. This was fate knocking at the door.

Patton replied that he could reassign three divisions. He would halt the movement of his 4th Armored Division to the east and have them stand by for further instructions; he would remove the 80th Division from the line and start them toward Luxembourg; and he would alert the 26th Division, though it had four thousand green replacements, to be ready to move in twenty-four hours. These three divisions were anywhere from seventy-five to one hundred miles from the southern flank of the German salient due north of them. Like most of Patton's troops, these divisions had been fighting fiercely and advancing swiftly for the last three months. They were weary, and now Patton would ask of them an unprecedented military feat.

After this meeting with Bradley, Patton and his key officers returned to Third Army headquarters at Metz. That night, about eleven o'clock, Patton's phone rang. It was Bradley. He instructed Patton to meet with Eisenhower and him at Verdun the next morning, December 19, at eleven o'clock. Patton then alerted his key staff officers to meet in his office in the morning at eight o'clock sharp. Patton opened the meeting by acknowledging they were all skilled at rapid movement, but that now they were going to have to really show what speed in battle could do.

He and his staff concocted a plan of attack with a few variables, to give Eisenhower three options. All three ended with Patton and his troops on the attack against the southern flank of the German salient. Before Patton and his staff officers left for Verdun, they cobbled together a simple code with General Gay, Patton's chief of staff, who would stay behind at Third Army headquarters and implement whatever option Eisenhower selected. At nine-fifteen Patton left for Verdun with two of his staff officers.

When they arrived at Verdun at ten-forty-five, they were ushered into a dank and cold squad room in an old barracks, heated only by a potbellied stove. Many of Eisenhower's key officers—Bradley, Devers, British air marshal Tedder, and others—were already there, seated around a large table. Patton and his men took their places at the table. The mood was glum. The Germans were succeeding, and the Allied officers seated at the conference table shared the responsibility for the total breakdown in Allied intelligence that had led to this embarrassment.

Eisenhower had designated General Strong, SHAEF G-2, to give an overview of the present situation in the Ardennes. Strong's report was grim and depressing. Eisenhower looked up and told everyone there would be no doom-and-gloom faces at this conference; the Germans had offered them a golden opportunity by abandoning their fortified defensive positions and coming out into the open on the offensive. Ignited by this declaration, Patton snapped that they should just let the Germans go all the way to Paris before they "cut 'em off and chew 'em up."

Like Eisenhower, Patton saw the mistake the Germans had made. By forging into the salient, creating the "bulge" that gave the battle its popular name, they had placed themselves in a forward position that was highly vulnerable to envelopment and annihilation. The German salient presented a smaller-scale version for encirclement than Patton's original grand plan of total encirclement of all German forces. Patton's new contingency plan was to attack the southern "nose" of their salient and to roll up their southern flank. This would trap the aggressors in the bulge and cut off their supply lines to the rear, depriving them of food, fuel, and ammunition.

Eisenhower looked at Patton and asked how soon he could

get to Luxembourg and assume control of the battle. Patton replied that he would be there that afternoon. Eisenhower then stated that he would like Patton to attack with no fewer than six divisions. Patton replied that he could attack the German southern flank with three divisions by December 23. That meant within four days—ninety-six short hours. Some of the other generals at the conference table laughed. To them Patton's reply was rash and impossible, especially given the vast distance between the German salient and the Third Army.

Patton did not laugh. Instead, he calmly laid out the contingency plans he had already set partially in motion to attack with only three divisions, the plans he had laid out to Bradley the day before. He told Eisenhower that waiting to attack with six divisions would take several more days and forfeit the advantage of surprise. Eisenhower listened, nodded, and then chose one of the options Patton had worked out that morning with his staff. Patton smiled his consent.

George S. Patton Jr. finally got what he had dreamed of all his life—the chance to rendezvous with destiny. He would attack the Germans as they were attacking, and he would vanquish them. Thirty years of studying and perfecting the techniques of mobile armored warfare were about to coalesce for him into the greatest tactical move of the Second World War. He would give the *Wehrmacht* a sample of *blitzkrieg* as he had mastered it.

That very morning, as Patton and his staff officers drove from Metz to Verdun, Eisenhower had pulled off another remarkable feat.

Because the cloud cover had held so thick and soupy, planes could not fly. So Eisenhower had commandeered all supply trucks and used them as troop transports to race the 101st Airborne about a hundred miles forward from Mourmelon in the rear echelon to the relief of Bastogne, where trapped American troops were fighting mightily to hold off German panzer divisions that had surrounded the town. Against great odds, these trapped American troops were defending Bastogne, and now the elite paratrooper division would join them.

After it was decided that the Third Army would attack, Eisenhower, Bradley, and Devers wrapped up the conference by detailing how the Seventh Army would hold the Third Army's forward positions in the south while the Third moved north. Then Patton called General Gay and conveyed the chosen battle plan via their code. Patton was delighted to know that his troops and tanks were already in motion. He prided himself on preparing his troops better than anyone. He insisted that all his men pass a basic test of covering a mile with a full battle pack in less than ten minutes, just as he insisted that they stay in shape. After all, he himself was fit, even in his sixtieth year. It was another way for him, like one of his heroes, Frederick the Great, to stay close to his troops. Similarly, he performed the tasks he required of his troops, sharing their risks in battle by riding forward in the saddle and inspecting the front lines in person. For all his vaunted military vanity, he generally kept himself approachable, on-site, and available. Right then he could not wait to join his men on the pending march north.

Patton left Verdun and spent the night of December 19 with his XX Corps in Thionville, just a few miles from the

Luxembourg border. He characterized the following day as "hectic." He drove from one position to another, checking on his troops and armor and huddling with his various commanders at all levels. On December 21, he received several phone calls from fellow generals admonishing him that attacking with only three divisions was unwise, too risky. They insisted it was better to wait, assemble six divisions, and advance in the security of numbers. Patton replied that it was always better to attack with a smaller force and achieve surprise than to delay while waiting for a larger force and then lose the element of surprise. For Patton this was bedrock philosophy.

On the third day, December 22, twenty-four hours ahead of schedule, Patton attacked the southern flank of the German salient with three divisions. He caught the enemy completely off guard. In a scant seventy-two hours he had moved his three divisions an average of seventy-five miles.

Patton's Third Army attack energized the American forces immediately. Word spread quickly that he had moved three divisions over a great distance to surprise the Germans. Such speed of movement had never seemed possible over such a large distance until then. Meanwhile, to the north, Eisenhower acted just as decisively and resourcefully. Within days, he poured men and matériel into the Ardennes; in one week he shifted 250,000 troops and 50,000 vehicles into the battle as it grew increasingly fierce.

Despite Patton's surprise attack on their southern flank, by Christmas the Germans were able to thrust the tip of their salient nearly sixty miles behind what had been, nine days earlier, the American front. They did this by counterattacking against Patton's attack and by driving forward north of it. The Allies were fortunate. On December 23, the skies cleared. Allied airpower came to the fore. The *Luftwaffe*, despite Hitler's assurances to his generals, did not answer the challenge. Railroads used by the Germans behind their lines to ship in troops and supplies were put out of commission at this crucial time. The panzer divisions encircling Bastogne were bombarded and strafed by fighters, to devastating psychological effect, as certain German commanders admitted after the war. Most important of all, the American C-47 transports were able to airlift and drop supplies into Bastogne— medicine, food, clothing and blankets, ammunition and artillery shells. These last two items were vital, for McAuliffe and his surrounded troops were running out of firepower.

On Christmas Day, the German commander of the vaunted Panzer Lehr Division, General Fritz Bayerlein, sent a small contingent of officers into Bastogne, waving a white flag, to demand that the Americans surrender. Reinvigorated by the airlift, Brigadier General Anthony McAuliffe of the 101st issued the most famous one-word reply to emerge from the war: "Nuts."

The next day, at two o'clock in the afternoon, General Gaffney called Patton and requested authorization to take a large risk with Combat Command "R," under Colonel Blanchard, and attempt a breakthrough to Bastogne. Predictably, Patton told him to proceed. Slightly less than five hours later Bastogne was liberated. But Blanchard and his troops managed to cut only a narrow corridor into the beleaguered town, merely three hundred yards wide.

The enveloping German forces did not desist over the next several days. Instead, they harassed and skirmished. Then on December 30, Patton launched an attack with his 11th Armored and 87th Infantry. His generals in charge had requested that he postpone it for twenty-four hours. He refused. When Patton's attack launched on schedule it immediately locked horns with a massive German counterattack spearheaded by the 130th Panzer Lehr Division and the 26th Volksgrenadier Division.

A standoff derailed both attacks, but fortunately for the Americans, Patton's timely attack broke up the German attempt to reseal the corridor into Bastogne. Had the Americans delayed their attack, the Germans would have isolated the town once again. Patton's embrace of Frederick the Great's twin mantras— "Audacity, audacity, always audacity!" and "Attack, attack, always attack!"—paid off for him and his men yet again, just as it had in North Africa, in Sicily, and in Normandy. Patton firmly believed that an army looking to dig in and hold position was an army waiting to be overrun, often digging its own grave. Above all else in warfare, he prized preparation, movement, speed, boldness, and firepower, looking always to advance. He maintained that this military philosophy led not only to victory but also to saved lives.

His attack on December 30 proved this philosophy. Not only did the Germans launch the counterattack that the 11th Armored and the 87th Infantry repulsed; they also attacked the north face of Bastogne and launched yet a third attack against Patton's forces northeast of Bastogne. In these additional two attacks, they deployed several other divisions. After the war, Patton characterized this German counterattack as the biggest that forces under his command had ever endured. He loved it that his men repulsed the enemy that fateful day and prevailed on all three fronts.

The previous day, the front page of the *New York Times* bore this headline: "Patton's Third Army Sent in Record Time to Halt Foe." The article said that the Battle of the Bulge had been ready-made for Patton because he was "an old cavalry hand who now is considered the world's foremost tank expert." As to the speed with which Patton stated he could attack the German salient, the article quoted one staff officer present at the Verdun meeting with Eisenhower: "It almost knocked me out of my chair." The article ended with a one-sentence paragraph that summed up Patton and the Third Army since they had landed in Normandy: "The restless three-star general who exploited Lieut. Gen. Omar Bradley's break-through at St. Lo [sic] and helped engineer the Falaise gap, which chewed the Seventh German Army to pieces, now is waging the kind of war that is to his own liking."

In *War as I Knew It*, Patton stated that during the desperate German counterattack on December 30, four Germans wearing American uniforms and driving a U.S. Army jeep were shot and killed. A similar incident that day witnessed a single sentinel spotting seventeen Germans in American uniforms, calling in reinforcements, and annihilating them. This would not have amused Eisenhower because Skorzeny's commandos had successfully spread the rumor of an assassination attempt aimed at him in his headquarters. The result was that Eisenhower was confined to quarters for security reasons, with a beefed-up security detail ensuring that neither Skorzeny nor any of his men could get through to the Supreme Allied Commander. In his ire at this enforced confinement while the battle raged, Eisenhower issued "Wanted Posters" featuring a picture of Skorzeny. He had copies circulated among all the Allied armies. Though Eisenhower was not amused at all this, many of the men under his command were, none more than his old friend Patton.

On a serious note, Eisenhower and Patton were delighted that Skorzeny's special troops were meeting such bitter ends. They were even more delighted that General Sepp Dietrich's Sixth German Army, the northernmost of the three attacking German armies, had been stymied by the bravery of the GIs of the American First and Ninth Armies. These GIs regrouped and fought back. Most important of all, after Peiper had refueled his tanks and armored vehicles on captured gasoline, he continued to the northwest. In doing this, he forced the U.S. 99th and 2nd Divisions to retreat back to the Elsenborn Ridge, the dominant physical redoubt between Peiper and his objective of reaching the Meuse in record time. The men of the 99th and the 2nd dug in and stymied Peiper, who was pushing his men, driving the tanks and armored vehicle column even at night, trying to close rapidly on their objective.

For several nights the GIs engaged Peiper's forces who were trying to advance with help from Dietrich's Sixth German Army. The temperature at night was well below freezing. Snow squalls blew against the faces of the combatants. The American GIs did not have winter clothing or uniforms. The Americans and Germans were fighting at such close quarters that hand-to-hand combat broke out in several locations. Still, the GIs held out. Eventually the Americans destroyed the three bridges at the town of Trois-Ponts that Peiper's forces needed to cross to reach the Meuse and advance on Antwerp. The Americans also managed to destroy the bridges behind Peiper that he and his tanks had already crossed, thus cutting off any chance of being resupplied. Also, the skies cleared sufficiently and Peiper's column, spread out behind him over twelve miles, found itself strafed and bombed by several squadrons of American P-47s. These aerial attacks cost Peiper many tanks and armored vehicles.

After the war Peiper stated that had he crossed the bridges at Trois-Ponts, he would have reached the Meuse within one day. From there it would not have been too difficult to turn north and race to Antwerp. As it was, he turned north in search of an intact bridge but found only heavy American resistance. After suffering American counterattacks for a few days at La Gleize, pinned down in the river valley, Peiper ran out of fuel and lost contact with other German units behind him. He had no other option but to abandon his vehicles and trek through the woods back toward the German lines. Otherwise he would have been encircled and captured.

The German failure in the north, coupled with Patton's relief of Bastogne, turned the tide of the greatest battle the U.S. Army had ever won. The subtitle of esteemed military biographer Carlo D'Este's book on Patton is "A Genius for War." Genius has always been described as inexplicable and indefinable. But it does have an ever-present hallmark. Patton, like all true geniuses, had but one overriding passion his entire life, and he pursued it with unstinting devotion. He wanted to be an immortally great military leader who kept his date with destiny. Although George S. Patton Jr. was terribly flawed as a man, he had few equals as a combat genius. The proof is that he succeeded at the Battle of the Bulge and kept his date with destiny by liberating Bastogne.

FOURTEEN

Bastogne and Beyond

AS USUAL, PATTON gave the credit for the phenomenal feat of relieving the siege of Bastogne and saving the American troops pinned down there to the soldiers and young officers of the Third Army. He did so publicly and in print, saying that he was only a hook to hang the Third Army on. He always knew there was enough credit to go around, and that most big deeds in life executed collectively came replete with enough credit for all participants to share. Vainglorious as he could be about military attire and proper dress, when it came to handing out plaudits he was never miserly and certainly never a credit-monger on his own behalf.

Fully aware of what his men had done in rescuing the troops trapped in Bastogne, he pronounced the feat unequaled in military history. It may have been. His troops had marched all that distance over icy and snowy roads, even at night, in the worst winter in Europe in half a century. None got lost. All made the appointed rendezvous, despite fresh snowfalls and frigid temperatures, especially after nightfall. All fought gallantly and breached the ring of battle-hardened German infantry and tankers surrounding the embattled town.

Even though the commanding officers of these enveloping German troops had demanded that the trapped American troops surrender unconditionally, no American commander had waved the white flag, aware that Patton's Third Army was on the way and believing that it would break through and rescue them, as indeed it did. Patton marveled at what American troops could accomplish, covering such a vast distance in execrable weather in less than seventy-two hours, and said publicly that his hat was off to them.

Of course, once Patton's men had driven the three-hundred-yard-wide corridor through the German lines around the town, giving the Americans access to resupply the trapped troops and move reinforcements and ammunition into the town, the Germans did not immediately relent. Instead, they tried to retake the town for days with assault after assault, all ultimately repulsed by the American defenders. By the end of the third day of these assaults, Patton was confident enough to write Beatrice that the relief of Bastogne was the outstanding achievement of the war.

In the face of his euphoria, Patton was quickly disappointed yet again by his commanders. Neither Bradley nor Eisenhower would listen to his entreaties to keep attacking and push rapidly to the east, driving the Germans back. As Patton had before, especially when he wanted to encircle the German forces trapped in Normandy by having Montgomery drive down on them from the north while he drove up on them from the south, thus encircling them in a pincer movement and trapping them west of the Seine, Patton now wanted to snare the Germans exposed in the salient, in the "bulge" itself.

Yet once again Bradley and Eisenhower, fearing the American troops had reached their limit of extraordinary effort, took their foot off the accelerator and lost the momentum Patton had built up with the Third Army's heroic rescue of Bastogne. For Bradley and Eisenhower, the victory at Bastogne was enough for now. For Patton it was not. He saw the opportunity to capture many German troops as they escaped to the east to fight another day, just as one hundred thousand Germans had escaped to the east after the battle of Normandy because the Allies had hesitated to close the noose on them. This kind of passivity bothered Patton not only for military but for humanitarian reasons as well. His philosophy was: when on the attack, stay on the attack. If you did not, you allowed the enemy the chance to regroup and set his defenses. This meant only one thing: you would suffer more casualties, including fatalities, for your own troops when you resumed the attack.

That is exactly what had happened when Patton was told to halt his advance to the east at the end of August, when he was within striking distance of the temporarily vulnerable Siegfried Line, before it had been reinforced. Such foolish loss of life pained Patton. He believed that attacking exposed men to the briefest interval of danger from enemy fire. Extending that interval of exposure through hesitation invited and incurred greater loss of life. Going on the defensive and digging in courted disaster, asked for annihilation, and, in his favorite ghastly metaphor, led to digging your own grave. He now thought Bradley and Eisenhower were repeating this very mistake. Patton knew that the Germans, though essentially beaten, were still fierce and effective fighters; the more time you gave them to dig in and defend, the more their prowess at defensive warfare would cost you, especially since the attackers had now turned invaders of the sacred fatherland, to be protected at all costs.

Subsequent losses over the next four months of heavy fighting would bear out Patton's predictions of how ferociously the Germans would defend their country when besieged by the Allies from the west and the Russians from the east. Allied casualties mounted steeply. Perhaps Patton also intuited that Bastogne marked the apex of his career, and that from here until the end of the war, which could not be too far off, he would experience only slogging combat and nothing like the exhilaration of slashing across France or the ecstasy of liberating Bastogne.

Not only did Bradley and Eisenhower forfeit the momentum of the spectacular feat of prevailing against steep odds at Bastogne, but, once the Allied armies resumed their eastward advance, they also reverted to giving preference to Montgomery and his 21st Army Group. It is always dismaying to read—with so many innocent young men's lives at stake—what a huge role politics and its vain pageantry plays in war whenever there is a coalition of nations fighting together. This wretched fact especially pained Patton, who despised the useless loss of life, considerations of his rivalry with Montgomery notwithstanding.

For political reasons, Eisenhower again acceded to the British desire to lead the triumphant defeat of Nazi Germany. Since Britain had stood alone against the Nazis before the Russians and the Americans were forced to join the fight against them, there was justification for the British wish to be seen in the vanguard of the armies that ultimately defeated them, but it undoubtedly would have been better, no matter who got the credit, to defeat them as quickly and expediently as possible with the least loss of life on either side of the conflict.

Patton was dismayed to witness preference yet again given to Montgomery. At one point Patton flatly refused to cede one of his armored divisions to Montgomery, and at another point he threatened to resign if he was to be ordered into a purely defensive stance. He wanted the Third Army to advance. Indeed it did. As he had throughout the Battle of the Bulge, he stayed highly visible to his troops through the eastward march on German soil itself, riding around in his jeep with the three stars on it, in his full uniform, identifying himself easily to enemy sharpshooters as the three-star general he was.

The fighting on German soil somewhat relieved his depression over Montgomery's ascendancy, and he took care of his men as always. Just as he had throughout the horrendous winter conditions of the Bulge, he insisted again on his troops having fresh, dry socks on a regular rotation to stave off trench foot, as deadly and debilitating to an advancing army as any heavy wound; and he ensured as well that his troops received hot meals on a regular basis, echoing his edict during the Bulge that every man receive a hot turkey dinner on Christmas.

After the Battle of the Bulge ended in the third week of January, Patton and his Third Army attacked the Eifel section of the Siegfried Line at the beginning of February. The fighting was brutal; once again, as in Lorraine, the terrain was not well suited to tank warfare. The weather was awful—mud, ice, sleet, and snow impeded rapid vehicle advance. Because of overcast skies, the tactical air wings could make few bombing runs to aid the advancing infantry and armor. The subfreezing temperatures were indescribably hard on the troops, and the dug-in Germans fought back hard. Progress was slow.

In the middle of February, Patton flew to Paris for a spell of rest and recreation but quickly returned to the front, remarking on the negative erotic effect of the total nudity of the Folies Bergere, leaving nothing, in his view, to the imagination. Then, on March 1, the Third Army took Trier, the capital city of the Eifel region. When Patton was reprimanded for advancing beyond his designated scope in capturing Trier, he insouciantly inquired if he should give it back—yet another instance of his crippling immaturity.

When word reached Patton six days later, on March 7, that troops and tanks from the 9th Armored Division, part of the First Army under Brigadier General William M. Hoge, famously captured the Ludendorff railway bridge at Remagen and crossed the

Rhine, he was elated that Americans had beaten Montgomery to the prize once again, as at Messina.

That same day, the Third Army covered fifty-five miles in forty-eight hours after Patton sensed an opening. The Third Army reached the Rhine at Coblenz but found its bridges destroyed by the retreating Germans. The six weeks expended by the Allied Armies to reach the Rhine had been extremely costly on both sides. Besides the heavy casualties taken by both sides, the Germans in that short span of a month and a half had lost a quarter million men as POWs.

At the end of that month, on March 31, when the Ninth Army on the north and the First Army on the south completed the encirclement of the Ruhr, trapping many German troops within its snare, Eisenhower issued a proclamation to all German troops and to the German people in general urging the soldiers to surrender and the people to plant crops. But the offer went unheeded, most likely from fear of Gestapo and SS retaliation and reprisals should the German soldiers or citizens have sensibly agreed.

Competitive as ever, during the night of March 22, Patton sneaked a Third Army division across the Rhine on bridges the army engineers had built, thus beating Montgomery across the sacred river of German mythology by a day. Predictably, Montgomery had been delayed in making his much-ballyhooed crossing by overly elaborate preparations for the momentous event. The next day Patton wrote a general order to all Third Army personnel, extolling their triumphs from the end of January up till then and assuring them that their assault in crossing the Rhine guaranteed even greater glory to come.

On March 24, Patton drove to the Rhine and crossed on the pontoon bridge, pausing in the middle to urinate into the fabled river, yet another instance of his immaturity, but one matched a few weeks later by an equally immature Winston Churchill. There would be still another regrettable lapse in judgment moments later when Patton reached the eastern bank and snatched up twin handfuls of dirt to emulate the action taken before the Battle of Hastings by William the Conqueror when he stumbled at Pevesney upon disembarking from his ship and setting foot for the first time on English soil. The Conqueror had flung the fist-fuls of dirt skyward in 1066. So now Patton, indulging empty gesture and over-the-top grandiosity, did the same thing in 1945.

Soon thereafter Patton made a serious mistake in judgment both militarily and personally. He sent a task force to rescue his son-in-law John Waters, who had been taken prisoner back in Tunisia when ordered to inspect the front lines. Patton had worried about him for the better part of two years and knew there was a fairly large POW camp at Hammelburg, forty miles behind enemy lines. Over the objections of two of his best subordinates, Generals Eddy and Hoge, Patton insisted that a task force be sent to rescue the denizens of this POW camp.

On the way in, things went well as Captain Abraham Baum led his men ruthlessly to the camp and liberated the prisoners, including Waters. But on the way back the Germans had mistaken the task force for the vanguard of a larger attack by the entire 4th Armored and so had directed elements of three divisions to converge on the area. Baum's task force was ambushed, and many men were lost; also, most of the temporarily liberated POWs were returned to captivity, including Waters, who would eventually make it out a month later to a hospital in London, where he was treated for a serious gun wound from a German sniper who shot him as he attempted to lead a surrender party from his new POW camp.

The operation was a fiasco that should never have been undertaken, especially since the liberation of the POW camp at Hammelburg would have been organically accomplished in a short while by the broad-front advance of the Allied forces. The loss of life he had caused pained Patton. When correspondents later asked Bradley if Patton would be reprimanded or disciplined for this costly misadventure, Bradley replied that the failure itself was punishment enough for Patton. Bradley, as so often before, had correctly read the chastised, embarrassed, penitent Patton.

But Patton was still Patton, with his compulsion to speak when he should be silent. In April, when General Manton Eddy and his VII Corps discovered the Reich's gold reserves and their stolen art treasures stored in the Merkers salt mine, Patton notified Bradley and Eisenhower, who duly showed up to inspect the mine and its contents. The three generals were lowered on an industrial elevator hung from a single winched cable. They had to descend twenty-one hundred feet underground. On the way down Patton insouciantly remarked that should the "clothesline" snap, promotions in the U.S. Army would be rapidly accelerated. Such gallows humor did not sit well with Eisenhower, who told

Patton to refrain from further remarks until they were back above ground. This was yet another instance of Patton giving voice to his omnipresent fear of death and trying with levity to defuse its debilitating impact on him.

But first and foremost he was always a warrior, and shortly thereafter in the early days of May, he was angered when ordered to halt the Third Army at Pilsen and not take Prague, a few miles away and yet another historical prize he coveted. That honor was to be accorded the Soviets, unjustly, in Patton's view, who saw the ceding of Central and Eastern Europe to the Soviet Union as a tragedy, an opinion many people would soon come to share, not least the majority of the Central and Eastern Europeans. A few days later the war ended on May 8, 1945.

Shortly thereafter so, too, did Patton's enjoyment of his career. His desire to be shifted rapidly by General Marshall to the Pacific Theater was denied. In the summer of 1945, he took a leave of absence from the Third Army and returned home to his family. In Boston he again put his foot in his mouth. At a gathering honoring him on the banks of the Charles River, he pointed to four hundred wounded former soldiers from the Third Army and declared them the real heroes. Only he did it clumsily and appeared to slight those who had lost their lives in the war. He was trying to rework his old inspirational theme to let the other guy die for his country, not you for yours, though he always phrased this belief in horrendous profanity.

Although he eschewed the profanity in Boston, his sentiment

came off wrong and caused a flap in which he seemed to denigrate the fallen. That was not his intention, but when Gold Star parents naturally protested, Patton found himself back in trouble with the brass. As usual he blamed the perfidious press, though throughout the war they had lauded him to the extent that he was now a national hero, even having appeared on the cover of *Time* magazine. This accounts for the hero's welcome he received when he left Boston and went to Denver and then on to his hometown hero's welcoming parade in Los Angeles.

Back in Germany in the fall as military governor and still head of the Third Army, now as a four-star general, Patton brought his character flaws with him and had to be relieved when he made intemperate remarks about the Soviets and also failed to implement the de-Nazification program swiftly and thoroughly enough. Eisenhower had to replace him in command with Patton's old friend and subordinate, Lieutenant General Lucian Truscott. Eisenhower assigned Patton to head up the Fifteenth Army, which was not really a proper army, but a unit designated to oversee the writing of the official U.S. Army history of World War II. George S. Patton Jr. had been put out to pasture.

As commander of the Fifteenth Army, he did his duty but planned to travel home to Massachusetts for Christmas 1945 and to not return again to Europe. He was not sure whether he could obtain a new stateside posting in the army or if he would simply have to retire from active service. When his friend and chief of staff Major General Hobart "Hap" Gay asked if he would like to do some pheasant hunting on Sunday, December 9, Patton readily agreed. That morning he and Gay got into the backseat of Patton's official

Cadillac sedan as Private First Class Horace L. Woodring climbed behind the wheel. They started the drive to the country fields they intended to hunt. Along the way a freight truck, making a left turn into a quartermaster's depot, pulled in front of the Cadillac.

A fender bender resulted. No one except Patton was hurt. Apparently his head whip-lashed against a lighting fixture in the ceiling of the passenger compartment, snapping the third vertebra of his spine and badly damaging the fourth, paralyzing him from the waist down. Immediately he recognized his condition from the difficulty he had breathing and moving his fingers. He remarked to General Gay on what an ironic way to die this would be after what he had gone through in his life as a combat soldier. His uncanny instinct, as usual, was on the money. Twelve days later, on Friday, December 21, an embolism struck his lung on the left side of his chest and induced heart failure, killing him quietly in his sleep at 5:50 p.m.

In his books on Patton, early biographer Ladislas Farago speculated on a possible assassination plot having ended Patton's life. As any reader of books on Europe in the immediate postwar years knows, anything was possible then. It really was the dark arena depicted so beautifully for all time by Carol Reed and Orson Welles in the incomparable movie *The Third Man*. Despite this postwar ambience of rampant skullduggery that pervaded Europe at the dawn of the cold war, most serious historians discredit such assassination theories, believing that Patton was the victim of a freak automobile accident.

Beatrice wanted him buried in the American cemetery in Luxembourg among other fallen members of his beloved Third Army, the command of which he claimed was the greatest privilege in his life. A simple white cross bearing the insignia of four stars marks his grave. The legend on the cross reads:

Geo. S. Patton Jr.
General. 02605. 3rd Army

Liberator of Bastogne George S. Patton Jr. pins the Distinguished Service Cross on Brigadier General Anthony C. McAuliffe, hero of Bastogne who, as commander of the 101st Airborne, refused to surrender the town to the Germans although surrounded and besieged by crack panzer divisions for ten grueling days.

General Patton's casket, mounted on a half-track, passes through the streets of Luxembourg on its way to interment at Hamm U.S. Military Cemetery, December 1945.

Legacy

GEORGE S. PATTON Jr. will be remembered chiefly for his triumphs in World War II as the best combat general the Allies had. Bastogne was clearly, as Patton well knew and stated, the outstanding tactical maneuver of the entire war. His campaign across Normandy in August 1944 was brilliant, especially the rapidity with which he moved two armored corps through Avranches-Pontaubault to spearhead General Bradley's Operation Cobra breakthrough. Speed also characterized his two-day march to the Rhine when he sensed the vulnerability at Coblenz. Even earlier, in Sicily, fast movement of armor and infantry highlighted his all-out thrust for Messina, despite his forces being technically in a supporting, not a leading, role.

His mastery of rapid armored warfare was second to none. His demonstration of the effectiveness of armor, artillery, infantry, and airpower combined in a coordinated assault lives on today in the U.S. Armed Forces. He is, in fact, the father of American tank warfare using combined weaponry, and as he accurately predicted to young officers during World War II, the future of warfare does reside principally in the use of effective airpower in all its manifestations.

As the father of American tank warfare, he left a legacy of excellence in training that is among the finest in United States military history. He established the Desert Training Center in Indio, California, that is still in use today, much expanded and enhanced. This training center is largely accountable for the excellence of rapid armored warfare as executed by the U.S. Army in Iraq in both 1991 and 2003. The successful tank campaigns there are also part of Patton's legacy. Techniques he developed and perfected in World War II were employed in Iraq on both occasions, highly refined and enhanced by modern technology. Interestingly, procedures established by Patton for the dissemination of training information and for equipping, evaluating, and educating personnel, especially tankers, are still in use by the U.S. Army.

He also left behind an example of command presence and effective leadership still valued and emulated by many officers in the U.S. Armed Forces. His emphasis on vocational professionalism in officers still rings true. His emphasis on aggressive offensive warfare and his disdain for defensive holding actions have also been adopted widely in the U.S. Armed Forces, as witnessed again in Operation Desert Storm in Iraq in 1991. Patton's contention that attacking armies incur fewer casualties had proved to be largely true.

★ ★ ★

Patton's positive legacy is offset, unfortunately, by his negative power of example, such as the infamous slapping incidents and his immature penchant for controversial political commentary, both within the military and in the wider geopolitical sphere. His contentiousness at times with other Allied commanders was also not to be emulated, as with Field Marshal Montgomery in Sicily and in northwest Europe, as well as with Air Marshal Arthur Coningham in Tunisia.

Yet these pronounced character failings of Patton's as a professional have to be offset with his great virtues as a man. When asked by a correspondent if it was true that he believed the corporal was the most important man in the U.S. Army, Patton replied that he did not believe so—before quickly adding that the private first class was. He valued his soldiers and lavished concern on them, though he was harsh on infractions, especially on any that threatened the lives of other men. When one of his commanding generals mishandled the traffic by having two armored divisions crisscross at an intersection, and as a result an MP was killed, Patton ordered the offending general to personally direct the traffic until the operation was over. To fulfill this order the general had to stand in bitter cold for nine hours, but Patton insisted on it, saying he could not tolerate the loss of another MP.

On the advance across Germany, Patton came upon a wounded soldier whose leg was horribly mangled. The man was clearly not going to make it. Patton stayed with the dying soldier until an ambulance arrived, talking to him and administering the morphine himself, a three-star general doing the work of a medic. This was proof that the man the perceptive Bradley had characterized as "softhearted" clearly was.

The same personality component would often be at work with the martinet Patton whenever it came to "boys being boys." Several times he busted his driver, the faithful Master Sergeant John L. Mims, back to private for his overindulgence in alcohol. Once Patton even drove them both back to headquarters after Mims drank himself cross-eyed in the hostess's kitchen at a cocktail reception for Patton in Knutsford. Before the papers demoting Mims could be fully processed, a stern Patton would always rebuke him, reminding him that it was unseemly for a three-star general to be driven around by a mere private. Then Patton would rescind the demotion, tear up the papers, restore the stripes, and put Mims back behind the wheel again.

Another time when Mims had gone on a bender and was incapacitated with what Patton called his "quarterly atrocity," a corporal was assigned to drive Patton's jeep. Patton, as he nearly always did, gave scant recognition to the wicked cold that day, wearing only his Eisenhower jacket over a sweater. When he noticed the young corporal was shivering and that his hands on the steering wheel were turning blue, Patton ordered him to stop. He then asked the young man if he had a warm sweater with him. He did not. Promptly Patton removed his sweater and ordered the corporal to put it on. Then they drove on.

As did Bradley, Eisenhower understood Patton's true nature, sensing that his bluster and showmanship as a martinet were a disguise for his softheartedness. In *Crusade in Europe* Eisenhower recalls a time when, to his everlasting amusement, he called Patton's bluff. Patton had appealed to Eisenhower for permission to discharge eighty of his officers for what he considered lack of execution and lack of aggression bordering on cowardice. Patton was incensed about this. Eisenhower agreed that they should go, but set one condition: he needed a written report from Patton laying out the reason for the dismissals. Week after week went by with a new excuse from Patton each time Eisenhower inquired where the report was. Finally things came to a head, and Eisenhower confronted Patton. Sheepishly, Patton admitted that he had reconsidered the entire matter and wanted no one discharged.

This was the true Patton he revealed to his wife, Beatrice, for forty-five years. Before an attack by the Third Army as the war wound down, on the eve of battle, Patton confided to her in a letter that he hated to think that young men under his command would die the next day. He told his wife that he wished instead he could fight singly to decide the issue, risking only his own life. Patton valued human life and sought to minimize its loss, even in war. Like Eisenhower, after the German defeat at the Battle of the Bulge, Patton, too, was distressed that the Germans would not surrender, but instead held out fanatically, costing serious wounds and deaths, all unnecessary, plus untold further destruction of property that was also totally avoidable.

Patton mourned the dislocation and pain he saw the German civilians suffer, many of them "peasants" who had nothing to do with calling this destruction down upon themselves. When he visited the concentration camps, despite his ingrained anti-Semitism, endemic in the American officer class at the time, he became enraged and then visibly sick, including vomiting, when viewing the horrors he had to witness. On another racist issue, even though Patton had the usual negative perceptions of blacks rife in his generation and class, he is not properly acknowledged for being the first U.S. Army officer to integrate his troops. He also awarded his African American troops decorations, commendations, and medals when they had earned them. In this regard he was much like another leader with Confederate roots and descended from a slaveholding family, President Harry S. Truman, who has never been given full credit for mandating, through legislation in the late 1940s, that all U.S. armed forces be fully integrated.

After the war, Patton's opponents and colleagues offered evaluations of his military and leadership abilities that summed him up pretty well. Von Rundstedt said simply that he was the best general the Allies had. Two of the commanding generals under von Rundstedt at the Battle of the Bulge, General von Manteuffel of the Fifth Panzer Army and General Brandenburger of the Seventh Army, praised Patton's skill in deploying speedy armored warfare, adding that he had mastered the leadership techniques necessary in this type of combat from the German model. Brandenburger also claimed that prior to the Battle of the Bulge he speculated that Patton would come up and attack the southern flank of the German salient. No one in the German high command took him seriously enough to pay any attention to his prediction, believing that the attack Patton did in fact carry out was highly unlikely because it was nearly impossible to accomplish with expediency.

As for Lieutenant General Hermann Balck's criticism of Patton's leadership and execution during the stalemate at Metz, it was a fight Patton would never have engaged in if given a choice. With proper clearances and supplies, especially gasoline for his tanks, he would have bypassed Metz as he had bypassed and then isolated the garrison at Rennes back in Brittany. Patton had nothing but contempt for bloodletting stalemates. World War I trench warfare had cured him of that fallacious battle philosophy, just as it had cured his friend Douglas MacArthur, whose island-hopping strategy was a species of *blitzkrieg at sea.*

Like MacArthur, Patton believed in enveloping and moving on, leaving enemy redoubts to die in isolation in his wake, cut off from supplies, ammunition, and food until, as with Rennes— and in fact what eventually happened at Metz too—the defenders simply surrendered. By the time Rennes surrendered, Patton and his Third Army were fighting in Germany. Should he have stayed and slugged it out there, too, as he was forced from above to do at Metz? Not hardly.

Any type of back-and-forth warfare was precisely the reason Patton took a jaundiced view of the costly and brutal fighting waged by the unimaginative and overly cautious and conservative Bradley and his friend Lieutenant General Courtney Hodges in the Hurtgen Forest with the First and Ninth Armies right before and during the Battle of the Bulge. This Hurtgen Forest fighting entailed much avoidable and wasteful loss of life. So intense was its savagery and so horrible its weather conditions that after the war it was compared to the worst fighting on the eastern front. To Patton it was a colossal waste. In his unwavering view, exposing one's troops to prolonged enemy fire led inevitably to unacceptable losses. He would have no part of it.

The best and most disinterested evaluation of Patton may have come from his old friend and former subordinate Lucian Truscott, with whom he clashed openly and bitterly in Sicily: "He was perhaps the most colorful, as he was certainly the most outstanding, battle leader of World War II." Most of the men who served under Patton took a similarly admiring view. Asked about their participation in the war, years after it ended, they would often simply reply: "I served with Patton."

The man who most benefited from Patton's genius for combat said the most revelatory thing about him. Eisenhower had deep powers of observation and evaluation when it came to other men. Realizing that Patton viewed his calling to military leadership as a vocation as sacred as that of the artist or the priest, Eisenhower said: "He was one of those men born to be a soldier."

That is why today there is the museum in his honor and the Armor School named after him at Fort Knox, Kentucky, and also why a larger-than-life statue of him stands outside the library at West Point, inscribed with the words:

> Pursue the Enemy with the Utmost Audacity
> and Do Not Take Counsel of Your Fears

Bibliography

Ambrose, Stephen E. *Citizen Soldiers: The U.S. Army from the Normandy Beaches to the Bulge to the Surrender of Germany, June 7, 1944–May 7, 1945.* New York: Simon & Schuster, 1997.

———. *D-Day: June 6, 1944: The Climactic Battle of World War II.* New York: Simon & Schuster, 1994.

Axelrod, Alan. *Patton: Lessons in Leadership.* New York: Palgrave Macmillan, a division of St. Martin's Press, 2006.

———. *Patton on Leadership: Strategic Lessons for Corporate Warfare.* New York: Prentice Hall Press, a division of Penguin Group USA, 1999.

Blumenson, Martin. *The Patton Papers: 1885–1940.* Vols 1 and 2. Boston: Houghton Mifflin Company, 1972.

D'Este, Carlo. *Patton: A Genius for War.* New York: Harper Collins Publishers, 1995.

Eisenhower, Dwight D. *Crusade in Europe: A Personal Account of World War II.* Garden City, New York: Doubleday & Company, Inc., 1948.

Farago, Ladislas. *Patton: Ordeal and Triumph.* New York: Ivan Obolensky, Inc., 1964.

———. *The Last Days of Patton.* New York: McGraw-Hill Book Company, 1981.

Hirshson, Stanley P. *General Patton: A Soldier's Life.* New York: Harper Collins Publishers, 2002.

Patton, George S. Jr. *War as I Knew It.* Boston: Houghton Mifflin Company, 1947.

Acknowledgments

WE THANK OUR agent, Alexander C. Hoyt, and our publisher, Joel Miller, without whose initiative and unfailing help this biography would not have been possible. Our editor, the gracious Stephen Mansfield, guided, exhorted, and edited us brilliantly. For his vital reading, commentary, suggestions, and direction, we salute our generous and talented friend Alexander Merrow. Congratulations and much gratitude are in order for Janene MacIvor, whose copy-editing was superb to the point of being stunning. Lisa Schmidt and Heather Skelton at Thomas Nelson Publishers were endlessly patient, thoroughly professional, and unfailingly helpful to us in every phase of book preparation and production.

Thanks are due also to the authors of the books listed in the bibliography for laying the foundation that made it possible for us to put this book together. Suggestions: For a brief yet excellent overview of Patton's life and career, read Alan Axelrod; for a thorough military biography, read Carlo D'Este; and for an in-depth academic and scholarly interpretation, read Stanley P. Hirshson. If you can, read all three. To gain an idea of Patton's writing style, voice, and personality, read the Martin Blumenson books, as well as Patton's own posthumous memoir, *War as I Knew It*.

For outstanding primary source research, Alexander Merrow and Tomoko Otsuka could not have been more effective. For essential and unstinting help with secondary source research, we thank the staff of the Heermance Memorial Library in Coxsackie, New York: Linda Deubert, Sandra Stephen, Jessica Kornheisl, Lynn Erceg, Lorri Field, Christine Reda, and Jacqueline Whitbred.

Candace Fuller at the George S. Patton Museum at Fort Knox guided us expertly to the rich trove of photographs in their archives, and Bill Chivil helped enormously with their selection and transmittal.

On September 27, 2009, an early autumn Sunday of warm rain in the Hudson River Valley, the late Corporal Albert Strausman of Brooklyn described in wrenching detail the savage fighting during the Battle of the Bulge amid nearly unendurable cold, snow, sleet, and freezing rain. At 8:30 in the evening on December 24, 1944 Al arrived at the front lines, and next morning he noted: "All the trees in the Ardennes had tin foil from the Germans dropping it to thwart Allied radar. It would be on the outer branches and looked like Christmas decorations." In later life a talented art teacher and accomplished sculptor, Albert was once wounded and twice decorated for his efforts, while still a teenager, during that epic battle: A Bronze Star for bravery under fire and a Purple Heart for a badly damaged leg, compliments of a German 88. Thanks, Albert.

About the Authors

AGOSTINO VON HASSELL is a writer and consultant living in New York and Virginia. He has published books on the United States Marine Corps, the West Point Military Academy, military food, modern piracy, and counter-terrorism. In addition he has worked as a chef and published many articles on the culinary arts. His website is www.agostinovonhassell.com.

ED BRESLIN IS a writer living in New York and the Hudson River Valley.